# WRESTLING WITH
# DEPRESSION

# WRESTLING WITH
# DEPRESSION

*A Spiritual
Guide to
Reclaiming
Life*

William and Lucy Hulme

**Augsburg**
MINNEAPOLIS

WRESTLING WITH DEPRESSION
A Spiritual Guide to Reclaiming Life

Scripture quotations unless otherwise noted are from the New Revised Standard Version Bible, copyright © 1989 by the Division of Christian Education of the National Council of the Churches of Christ in the U.S.A. and used by permission.

Scripture quotations noted RSV are from the Revised Standard Version Bible, copyright © 1946, 1952, 1971 by the Division of Christian Education of the National Council of the Churches of Christ in the U.S.A. Used by permission.

Cover design by Craig P. Claeys
Interior design by Elizabeth Boyce

Library of Congress Cataloging-in-Publication Data

Hulme, William Edward, 1920-1995.
              Wrestling with depression : a spiritual guide to reclaiming life /
    William and Lucy Hulme.
                     p.   cm.
              Includes bibliographical references.
              ISBN 0-8066-2699-2 (alk. paper)
                1. Depressed persons—Religious life.   2. Depression, Mental—
    Religious aspects—Christianity.   3. Depression, Mental—Case
    studies.   4. Hulme, William Edward, 1920-1995.   I. Hulme, Lucy.
    II. Title.
    BV4910.34.H85   1995
    248.8'6--dc20                                 95-22352
                                                    CIP

The paper used in this publication meets the minimum requirements of American National Standard for Information Sciences—Permanence of Paper for Printed Library Materials, ANSI Z329.48-1984. ∞

Manufactured in the U.S.A.                                     AF 9-2699

99    98    97    96    95    1    2    3    4    5    6    7    8    9    10

# CONTENTS

# ONE

## *It Can Happen to You*

HAD I DIED SHORTLY before my seventieth birth-day, I would never have known a depression. It was the last thing that I anticipated. Nevertheless it hit me—and hit me hard. From the beginning I felt helpless before its onslaught. I knew it was not an ordinary down mood—those I had experienced. This was something beyond my every experience and imagination. It sent me to the mental illness units at the University of Minnesota Hospital where I remained for two and a half months. There I experienced one of the worst depressions that hospital had ever treated. I recall that when I first arrived at the hospital I told my wife, Lucy, that trying to end this depression would be like trying to stop a moving freight train with my bare hands.

Being a professor of pastoral care, I not only knew a great deal about depression academically, but also vicariously through the many people with depression I had counseled. In my professional life, I had rubbed shoulders with the mental health professionals in our community, including the psychiatrists who taught at the university's department of medicine. In fact, I had met with their faculty of psychiatry just a few years previously as we set up a cooperative program for our graduate theological students in pastoral care to take a course in the department of psychiatry. I doubt that they ever expected to see me as a patient in the hospital. I was informed that if it could happen to me, it could happen to anyone.

Because it can happen to anyone, I decided to tell my story in the hope that should it happen to you or to a family member, you will know what to do. Depression is our most common mental illness and is widespread in our society. It is no respecter of persons, hitting rich and poor, white and black, men and women (although in our society there are twice as many women as men who are depressed), religious and nonreligious, those who practice self-care and those who do not.

## A BOUT WITH PNEUMONIA

Some physical diseases have a statistical relationship with the onset of depression. I believe pneumonia precipitated my depression. At the time, I was fulfilling a speaking engagement at my alma mater and at first felt fine. But toward the end of my stay, I noticed that I wasn't feeling well, and I hoped I could get home before I got any worse. When I returned home, I said to Lucy that although I had never had the flu, I was experiencing what other people said the flu felt like. She advised me to go to bed, which I did. When I felt no better after one day's rest, I stayed in bed another day. Still no better, I saw my doctor who, after listening to my lungs, said I did not have pneumonia, but rather the flu. Later when I still felt no better, she admitted me to the hospital. There, through X rays, it was discovered that I had a very severe case of pneumonia, even though no one was ever able to hear anything in my lungs.

By this time the memory of my mother's death began to preoccupy me. She died of pneumonia after her physicians believed she was improving. But she had a premonition that she would die, and her doctor told me that physicians can feel powerless when faced with such states of mind. Now I began to get that same premonition. I was concerned that I would not leave the hospital alive. I saw myself being carried out as a corpse. Along with the premonition, I began to feel depressed. I requested that there be no visitors, although I did ask to see a few people. I was seeking spiritual help and told each of these persons, including my pastoral counselor, Bill Smith, that I was depressed. For three weeks I was given the most powerful intravenous antibiotics available because my pneumonia had become life threatening.

When the people whom I had requested to see would come, I would hand them my Bible and ask them to read. I was hoping for help through my faith. My greatest fear was of the nights because I wasn't sleeping. Rather, I continually suffered the psychic pain of depression, which seemed never to leave or abate. I saw it as never ending—a typical sign of depression. I kept losing weight, which became obvious each day as I was weighed on scales brought to my bed. So I overate, not because I was hungry or enjoyed the food, but to try to reverse what to me was a downhill slide.

But the puzzling thing about my condition was that even when my pneumonia began to improve, my white blood cell count remained high. Suspecting something else was involved, doctors did a bone-marrow biopsy, which revealed, somewhat inconclusively, that I had chronic leukemia.

After three weeks I was able to leave the hospital with the provision that Lucy would administer the antibiotics intravenously to me at home. I can recall telling myself as I left the hospital that I wasn't really leaving. The premonition was still in full gear.

## Sent Home to Recover

At home the depression continued, although as long as we both had to concentrate on the administering of the intravenous antibiotics, it remained under control. While receiving the antibiotics, I had to watch that I received just so many drops a minute; my attention was needed because sometimes the drops would stop. I had to keep my mind on what was going on. We did this treatment twice a day. During the week of intravenous treatments, I also tried a couple other tasks. At Lucy's request, I cut up cardboard boxes and tied them together for recycling.

I did the work fairly well, although it took longer than usual. I recall a feeling of satisfaction that I could do it. I also tried to do some copying at a copy machine that needed coins. There I became terribly confused. I kept ruining copies and having to get more change. The task took me at least three times as long as usual. I recall driving home feeling disturbed by the experience. I drove just a short distance, yet I was relieved when I returned home because I did not feel safe driving.

One day during that week, Lucy was hesitant to leave me home alone when she went to work so she took me to her college, where I stayed in the refectory. I had my lunch there as I waited for her return. I recall this as a horrible experience. With all the students coming and going, the pain increased to a degree that seemed intolerable because I could not relate to any of those busy students.

At the end of the week, when the visiting nurse said that I no longer needed the antibiotics, I slipped badly into my depression. Without the structure that the intravenous treatments provided, the depression went into high gear. I suppose in retrospect that the whole process had helped me to hold onto some responsible activity. I have discovered since then that having a structure for daily living is an antidote to depression.

## TO THE PSYCHIATRIC UNIT OF THE HOSPITAL

During the week of intravenous treatments, I talked with my pastoral counselor, Bill Smith, regularly. When the depression became significantly worse after the end of the antibiotics, I called him. Although we had previously agreed that I would not go to the hospital, that night Bill saw that I needed to go. At Lucy's suggestion, I called Ted Arneson, who had connections with the University of Minnesota Hospital. I had counseled Ted when he had battled a severe depression. He had subsequently been a patient at the university hospital where he had been cured by shock treatments. Although it was late at night, Ted and his wife, Ruth, came right over. He too was soon convinced that I needed to go to the hospital. He called the head of the department of psychiatry at the university, probably getting her out of bed. After talking to me, she too said that I should go to the hospital and that she would arrange for a bed for me. I reluctantly agreed to go.

After Ted had taken me to the hospital, I had second thoughts and was ready to leave, but Ted reminded me that I had been in bad shape at home and would be returning to that state. I also thought of Lucy, that it would be too much for her if I returned, so I stayed.

Because it was the middle of the night, I was placed with another patient. I had a fear of sharing a room so I used my influence with the hospital chaplain, whom I knew, to get me a private room. As long as I was in that unit, I had a room to myself. Whether it would have made any difference if I had had a roommate, I do not know.

I went to the hospital as much to relieve Lucy of my constant and painful presence (which must have been most wearing) as to get help for myself. By now I was seriously doubting that I could receive any help. But I could no longer tolerate the thought of going back home that night.

Before I had left home for the hospital, I told Lucy that I didn't want to go because I knew they would want to shock me. I was well educated in the treatment of depression and had even previously viewed a University of Minnesota film on modern shock treatments. I knew of their great improvement over the past, but I still feared them.

## The Prescription for Shock Treatments

On my second day in the hospital, I was taken to a conference of psychiatrists. There, after interviewing me, they informed me that cognitive behavioral therapy was not applicable to my depression and that medication would function too slowly for me. So, they said, the needed treatment for me was electroconvulsive therapy (ECT) or shock treatments. My reaction to this recommendation was to say, "Give me something instead to help me sleep." They told me bluntly that there was nothing that could do that. "Knock out the depression," they said, "and you will sleep."

The medications that the psychiatrists believed would be "too slow" in my case normally take six weeks to be effective. This shows the urgency with which they viewed my condition. In their opinion, I simply couldn't wait that long.

In Minnesota, and I believe generally, a patient has to sign permission to receive shock treatments. When my psychiatrist and his associate came to me with the paper to sign, I was reluctant. Under their pressure, I agreed to sign but with the provision that I could back out. They agreed, I suppose because they saw that this was the only way they could get me to sign.

This occurred on a Friday. Shock treatments were given Monday, Wednesday, and Friday mornings. That weekend I developed a 102 degree fever and a swollen hand so my first treatment, which was supposed to have been on Monday, was postponed to Wednesday. On Saturday evening I was transferred, despite my protests, to the general hospital hematology unit where I was diagnosed with gout. My general hospital room was very large and I had it to myself. I stayed there two days and two nights. There I went downhill fast. I was left alone in the room and nurses rarely checked on me, I suppose because I really wasn't their patient. The continuous activity of the mental unit to which I had become accustomed was missing. The last night there I had hallucinations in which I saw my whole family rejecting me. I also imagined myself trapped in the hospital forever. I would never get out. It was a wild night.

When the phone rang the next morning and I knew it was Lucy, I didn't answer it because I believed that she hated me. When she came, I told her I was surprised that she would come. I told her that day that I was not going to take shock treatments.

When I returned to the psychiatric unit, I was placed in a different room with a roommate. Again I persuaded the chaplain to use his influence to get me a single room. It was while I was in a panic about being in the same room with someone that I recall Lucy saying, "Now I know you really need shock treatments."

Shock treatments were something members of my family were at first reluctant for me to have because of their antiquated impressions about them. But as my condition worsened, everybody except me wanted me to have such treatments.

When the Monday morning came when the treatments were scheduled to begin, Ted Arneson, Bill Smith, and Lucy were all in my room to see to it that I went when my turn was called. But to no avail. They tried every way—verbal persuasion, pleading—and when these failed, they physically dragged me to the door of the shock treatment room. Bill even had me halfway inside when the psychiatrist in charge rebuked him—reminding him that he was breaking the law. I wrenched myself loose and went back to my room.

Now what to do with me? I thought the hospital would dismiss me. I recall hearing my psychiatrist apologize to the shock treatment psychiatrist for my behavior. What happened next was for me totally unexpected. Lucy and a team of psychiatrists entered my room and informed me that they were taking me to court.

I will pause here so that Lucy can tell her experiences. In these first chapters where I tell what happened to me, Lucy will follow with her story. My impressions are not sufficient to describe what she went through. Another reason to hear her story is that families of depressed persons are often neglected in the care that they need.

## Lucy's story

Our family, similar to other families where one person is depressed, had many needs. As Bill's wife I realized that I needed to recognize and not deny the symptoms.

Given our society's bias and misinformation about severe depression, families like ours are confronted with a new and difficult situation when a member becomes depressed. When the illness begins, a family observes new, often strange behavior from a formerly normal person. Family members do not know what to expect. They are faced with a completely foreign and patternless progression of events. For our family, we knew that we should be open as much as possible and in no way be untruthful.

So I will tell my story. Had it had a different outcome, I do not know whether I could or not.

## Experiences at the Beginning

In the background of the day-to-day hospital visits was my faith that I was in God's care. Day after day with Bill, I was confronted with the fact that there was no improvement in any area. I knew that I had to be vigilant to observe any change. I was always aware of my role as informed observer. As nothing could be taken for granted, I lived on a plane of heightened awareness. I trusted in my basic humanity and believed that I would be guided in the right way. This was new territory for me, but I was "old" to myself. I had read extensively about mental illness as it is popularized in magazines and newspapers, but this was the first time I had visited anyone in a mental hospital. I had much to learn.

One of our friends warned me that compared with other facilities, the University of Minnesota Hospital was not very "nice." I had nothing to compare it with and so when I found Bill's care quite competent and his room adequate, I was satisfied. He really could not have had better surroundings at this time. His being safe was my main concern. I thought my life experiences would let me know if his environment was harmful or not, and I believe they did at the time.

I also had concerns about my own health. Because I needed a hip replacement, one of my immediate concerns was how to shorten the distance from the car to Bill's bed. My going back and forth to the hospital became a time for me to ponder my religious faith and philosophy of life and their meaning for the present crisis. Although I could become exhausted, I always seemed to have the energy to keep alert. With my painful hip, the exertion of the walk to Bill's room from the parking ramp, and sometimes having to climb three flights of stairs when the elevator was out of order, meant that when I went to bed at night I slept soundly and seemed to know that I was doing all I could. So I was not agitated during my sleep.

I continually prayed for any guidance. I desperately wanted to know if there was anything more that I could do. I made calls to agencies for information, following up any lead and calling any person who I thought might have insights. I researched at the university's medical library and talked to anyone who might have a shred of information, whether they were high or low on the totem pole. I knew that when one needs information, it may come from a strange place.

## BEING TRUTHFUL, BEING CAREFUL

I did not attend church after the first couple Sundays of Bill's hospitalization. He was very well known in the church and I would have found having to answer all the questions wearing and not helpful. "How is he getting along?" "No, he is no better." "What do his doctors say?" And on and on. Many of the questions were not helpful; people would press for details they did not need. To me this seemed offensive. I also observed with my rational mind that many of these people were asking for themselves, as they were or had been depressed. Some were just morbidly curious. Some offered reassurances that they were in no position to offer; they rather needed to reaffirm their positive religious hope. Because of my age and experience, I did not let other people's reactions become anything further than a momentary annoyance. As church people, they really did mean well.

I did not feel I could give the details of Bill's condition because they would be too shocking to anyone who knew Bill. The state he was in could have led them to conclude that he could never recover. I also did not know whether he would recover or not, but since the doctors from the university who were at the top in their profession said he would recover, I held to this. I could not let others have the whole picture because they would not have been able to erase that impression when and if he became well. So I did not say more than, "He is in a fine hospital and I have confidence in the doctors. He is being treated for depression."

The family was permitted to deny visitors to Bill. With his being completely delusional and deranged and apathetic, the total opposite of his usual self, I felt I could not allow any visitors. Anyone coming to the unit was turned away. If I happened to be there, I told them that he did not want any visitors, which was also true. I would visit briefly with them and send them on their way.

Once or twice a person slipped in and those persons were usually not the type who were helpful as visitors. I still believe that allowing no visitors was the best procedure, for Bill's future relationships and reputation as a clergyman could have been jeopardized.

## LEARNING MORE ABOUT DEPRESSION

Each chapter will include a section of practical information on depression and related issues that we hope will help you to both understand depression and to know what to do when it occurs. In this first chapter, we will describe some varieties and causes of depression, list some of its symptoms, and discuss the importance of recognizing these symptoms.

### Varieties and Causes of Depression

*Clinical, Chronic, and Situational Depressions*

My major depression was a clinical depression. It was a medical problem requiring medical intervention and could have been called a "brain disease." No verbal therapies were helpful. If you or someone you know has had a depression, it is quite likely that it was not as severe as mine. You may find that you have problems identifying with me as I tell about my clinical depression because of its severity and because of the psychotic symptoms that I experienced.

More than a year later, I experienced a mild depression after I had contracted incurable Ménière's disease, which I describe in chapter four. That is the one you are more likely to identify with. It could be called a situational depression because a specific situation triggered the depression. Situational depressions are triggered by major losses, disappointments, or other traumas. In my case, it was the persistent vertigo from Ménière's disease. After a time, the depression itself can become the trauma as the original trigger slips into the background. One of the first symptoms of depression is reading "foreverness" into the trauma. Hope begins to vanish. In my case, that foreverness had a rational base, which only exacerbated my reaction.

Most depressions are of the moderate sort I had with my situational depression. Other moderate depressions are not as much situational as chronic. The body chemistry of some people is such that they tend to feel sad and depressed more often than others. Sometimes medications are needed, at least for a time; a section on helpful medications is included in chapter four. Chronic depressions are longer lasting but not necessarily severe.

Some people are chronically depressed, seemingly never knowing happiness. That was the case with a former student of mine. I happened to see him at a conference about fifteen years after his graduation from seminary. "I have something to tell you," he said. "Last year when things got beyond the tolerable point for me, I went to a counselor. He sensed I was depressed, and in our conversation, it soon became apparent to me that I have been depressed all of my life. He finally helped me deal with some things I had continually avoided. It took several months, but I finally came out of the depression. I now know life as I have never known it before and it's wonderful!"

I must confess that in all the time I had him as a student, I never perceived his depression. I felt so good hearing his story that I didn't ask him further questions concerning his psychotherapy. But one thing he said led me to believe that learning to face and express his anger might have been a part of it.

He grew up in a parsonage and said this about his father: "In my family, my dad could get angry, but no one else."

Other people have recurring bouts of sadness or melancholy. They are not in terror or even in any great anxiety. Rather, they are locked into sadness. Others have Seasonal Affect Disorder (SAD). They become depressed in the bleak winter months and feel better with the coming of the brightness of spring. For some, light is therapy for depression and getting extra doses of light during bleak periods may help.

As will be described later, some people, particularly women, have a physiological cycle that brings on depression, such as PMS (premenstrual syndrome). Those with such physiological cycles usually learn to live with them, knowing that the depression will leave when their physiology changes.

Situational depressions, at least as they begin, have their origin in one's reaction to a negative experience. That is different from clinical depressions and most chronic depressions where the origin lies in a chemical imbalance in the brain; it is primarily physiological. As a situational depression continues, it may develop a physiological component if it persists; it can apparently create a chemical imbalance in the brain. When that happens, a physician can prescribe medication to help the depressed person.

Many situational depressions have their roots in grief. The normal reaction to a significant loss is grief. Following the loss of a loved one, a significant job, a bodily function, or the dissolution of a marriage, one grieves. While grieving has some similarities to depression, it is not depression. However, it can turn into depression if the grief work is not done.

Grieving people need to express their feelings and tell their memories to others. Doing so helps grief to resolve itself over a period of time. But those who seek to avoid dealing with the pain of grief by attempting to lose themselves in their work or in other ways are the ones who are likely to become depressed.

If you have suffered a loss, seek out those people with whom you can talk and regularly share your feelings. If it is a loved one who has died, talk about him or her to others. Share your memories. If people you know are grieving, be persistent in reaching out to them and in helping them express their feelings and talk about their memories. You will be aiding them to grieve in a healthy way and sparing them the possibility that their grief will turn into depression.

*Differences and Similarities among Depressions*

Though depressions are different in degree, the clinical being the more intense in its anguish, they are also different in kind. In clinical depression, one can enter insanity as I did, living in a world of delusion. The dividing line between the varieties of depression can be hazy, however, because when a situational or chronic depression increases in intensity, it may develop into a clinical depression. This is not inevitable, however, no matter how long the depression may last. But if and when it does happen, helplessness and hopelessness become total, and one is not only dysfunctional but immobilized. Originally a person may have had some kind of medical problem and perhaps had it before, but now the disorder is completely a medical problem.

All depressions have some things in common, with the more serious depressions being intensifications of the mild. Because these symptoms are not often recognized, even by professional care givers, we will take a look at them.

## SYMPTOMS OF DEPRESSION

Recent studies have shown that many physicians do not often recognize the symptoms of depression in their patients. This is unfortunate because the physician is the one that depressed people often turn to because their depression is masked behind their physical symptoms. In order for depression to be treated, it must first be recognized.

Depression, depending on its intensity and severity, can be hellish, a trauma in which one is both miserable and overcome with feelings of helplessness, powerlessness, and hopelessness. Depression is often observed first by those who live with or know the depressed person. They notice deviations from the person's usual behavior patterns. When I asked the wife of a man I was counseling how she knew her husband was depressed, she said she could tell because he had grown quiet and withdrawn, different from his usual self.

## Sleep

Another way depression can be spotted by observers is when there is a disruption in a person's normal sleep patterns. Usually this means the person has difficulty sleeping, is up often at night, wakes too early in the morning, and begins to show signs of sleep deprivation. A few people go to the other extreme and greatly increase their sleeping time. Just prior to my cousin's son's suicide, in his depression, he was staying in bed most of the day.

## Food

Another characteristic to watch for is a deviation from normal appetite patterns. Usually this involves a loss of interest in eating. Food is no longer appealing and there is no hunger. But some go in the opposite direction. They overeat, particularly sweets, as though they are trying to find some pleasure through taste, a brief escape from their miserable feelings.

## Simple enjoyments

Another symptom is a loss of enjoyment in the normal pleasures of life. A spouse may notice his or her partner growing less interested in sex, and perhaps even withdrawing from it. Hobbies that once held one's interest no longer do. Devotees to watching sports on television may even cease to turn on the set.

## Mental slowdown

Perhaps due to the intensity of the psychic pain that never leaves and sometimes never even abates, the depressed person is mentally reduced. It takes longer to do even simple tasks and one usually doesn't do them as well as previously. Memory frequently fails. During my clinical depression, I felt strongly that I was losing my memory, and it wasn't all delusion. I recall on many occasions trying to retain my memory by seeing how many of my fifty-four colleagues' names I could remember. Outside of the four in my department, I could remember only four other names. I kept repeating those four as an exercise to keep what little memory I had left.

### Frustration

Also in depression one has a very low threshold for frustration. Simple problems can frustrate a person and it is very difficult to be persistent. As one's self-image plummets, one can feel totally worthless, no good, a predestined failure in every way.

### Fatigue

Depressions drain one of energy. One experiences fatigue, often feeling the need to lie down and sometimes to stay down. Chronic fatigue syndrome may be related to this facet of depression. I often found in my counseling that those diagnosed with chronic fatigue syndrome were often also suffering from depression.

### Difficulty facing the morning

Depressed people find it difficult to face another day. Morning is the worst time for many. They find it difficult to get up and to think about another doleful, frightening day ahead. Through this focus and feeding on the fears of depression, they dig the hole deeper for the day as they ingest their depressed thoughts into their spirits. For many, the morning has often been preceded by a sleepless or even terrifying night; or perhaps they have escaped through sleep and do not care to awaken. During the day, depending on whether they are continuing with their work obligations, they may not perform well because their concentration is scattered by their preoccupation with their depression. Caring and concerned employers will keep them on even when they are not really earning their pay, although some employers may not be financially able to do this. Working is good because this involvement, no matter how minimal, is better than no involvement and is to some degree therapeutic.

## Emotional turmoil

A depressed person may appear sad, and is sad. The old word for depression was melancholia. As a child, I recall hearing my family talk about my uncle's repeated bouts of melancholia. While depression is really its own emotion, anxiety is perhaps the most dominant conscious experience. One is scared. Fear can turn into terror as the depression intensifies. For some, the dominant conscious experience is sadness. Although a depressed person can look phlegmatic and unemotional, he or she is churning with agitation within. The outward look is deceiving. One can also appear cross. I know that others, particularly the hospital staff, saw me in this way. Anger is also often part of depression. Many times it is repressed, but it can often come out as annoyance or irritability.

## Reduced social contacts

In line with the general slowdown, a depressed person's involvement in relationships is subdued. Depressed persons are often quiet in the company of others, speaking only when spoken to. Their mood is the opposite of enthusiasm. Often they look for ways to avoid social contacts.

## Self-criticism

Even when not depressed, we have a tendency to internalize other people's criticisms of us. During depression this tendency increases tenfold. Such internalization has a long history, going back to parental and sibling criticism of us as children. When we hear it often enough as children, we tend to believe the criticism as an accurate evaluation, and soon it becomes our own. Since depressed persons have confirmed these old criticisms as true, they become their own judges. In this regard, depression can be a form of self-punishment, however subconsciously or involuntarily administered. These self-judgments are a way of flagellating ourselves.

*Criticism from others*

Since depressed people are prone to being highly self-critical, they are very vulnerable to criticism from others. They sink under it because it adds to the weight of their already low self-image. Yet by not pulling their weight, withholding initiative, and being insensitive to other's needs, they invite criticism. The hospital staff was having problems finding veins to attach my intravenous tube for liquids; they continually failed. They even tried to find a vein on my toes. All during this, one of the psychiatric nurses kept saying, "Well, it's your fault. If you would drink, we would not have to do this." That was not the thing to say to a depressed person who had no recourse with his delusional system except not to drink. She was treating me as though I were a responsible person, which I was not. The incident stands out as one of the most miserable times I had in the hospital.

I am sure I annoyed the staff many times. After I was well, I asked my psychiatrist, Dr. Bill Sheehan, if he was ever angry with me. He paused a moment and then said, "No, not angry. But frustrated? Yes!"

## Recognizing the Symptoms

If these symptoms are apparent to you or your friends or loved ones, it is important that you recognize them as indicative of depression. Not all depressed people have all of the symptoms, but all have some. When we recognize these symptoms in ourselves or others, we need to get ourselves or others to the best available treatment. Depression affects 11 million adults a year and is responsible for 20,000 suicides a year. This latter figure alone is enough to motivate us to act.

Physicians are among the first to see the signs of depression because people come in to ask about other ailments that may be related to the depression. Yet only one-third of these patients are appropriately diagnosed and treated. Dr. John Ruth, who co-chaired a panel discussing this subject, spent three years studying this problem. He said, "Depression is not a down time. It is a disorder." He went on to say that depression costs the United States 27 billion dollars a year, of which 17 billion is due to lost work. The panel's goal is to help physicians recognize these symptoms in their patients ("Doctors Urged to Look for Signs of Depression," *New York Times*, April 21, 1993).

So going to your doctor may not be the best way to get help for yourself or your loved ones. Seek out a psychiatrist or clinical psychologist whose training is in the area of mental illness. You should also see your pastor, both for the spiritual help he or she can give and for the best referral to a health care professional.

# Two

## A Deepening Depression

 GOING TO COURT PROLONGED my hospital stay by a month. That is how long it took before my first court appearance. During that time I degenerated much further. Our family became convinced that such delays are one of the problems with court referrals.

### THE DELUSIONS

During that time of waiting, my delusions greatly increased. One might call my initial premonition when I had had pneumonia a delusion, but it was mild compared to the delusions that followed.

Hospitals are the place to go to get the care and treatments that one cannot get at home. Otherwise most of them are not conducive to healing. Shortly after my refusal to take shock treatments, I had an experience in the middle of the night that I thought meant the end of my kidneys. I was convinced by a feeling in the area of my kidneys after urination that they had completely collapsed. After that I refused all liquids because I was absolutely sure that they would not go through. I also believed that peristalsis had ceased in my intestines and consequently I refused to eat anything on the conviction that the food would simply pile up in my abdomen and surgery would be required to remove it.

When my refusal to eat and drink became critical, I was moved, again at midnight, from the unit for the mildly disturbed to the one for the severely disturbed. There I was given liquids intravenously.

Finally as my physical condition worsened, the psychiatrist, under prodding from Lucy, decided he had to place a tube down my nose into my esophagus. I recall this as a terribly painful experience. The nasal passage must have many sensitive nerves because passing the tube through caused excruciating pain. Because of my reaction to the pain, I don't believe they got the tube down as far as they desired. From then on, I was fed by liquid through this tube. Having the tube always in my throat was most uncomfortable. It seemed there was not room for me to breathe or to swallow my saliva.

I began to believe—without a doubt—that I was all-powerful in a destructive way, that I could and would destroy people. I took a perverse delight in seeing in my imagination my family as depressed as I was, with tubes up their noses, homeless on the street, where I was convinced they would end up. This was my power over them. Yet I was ambivalent. I believed that if they didn't come to see me, they might be spared. So I asked them—commanded them—not to visit me, ever! I recall telling my son Dale and daughter-in-law Sue that I was the archfiend of the universe. I saw myself as totally evil.

At first I held to a minimal faith in God, but soon lost it to the delusion that I was damned—again without a doubt. I believed this very strongly. I also believed that I would end up as a street person with a tube in my nose, a prey to tormentors. On at least two occasions, I lay in my bed, petrified with fear, because I was convinced that I would be attacked by the other patients, some of them quite wild, as the staff turned me over to them to be tormented and abused. The delusion was aided by the unit I was in. It was full of severely disturbed people who were shouting, cursing, wailing, and shrieking much of the time, especially during the night. Many times orderlies had to quickly surround and subdue a patient. Because my door was never allowed to be closed, I saw and heard all of this.

My son-in-law Paul recalls my warning him about a plan of destruction against him and my daughter Marcia. I told him that they would have to be careful because people were plotting against them. Paul replied that they were not in any trouble and were doing just fine. I was quiet for a moment and then said that there was a master plan out there to get all of us. Paul then said, "What you are saying is not logical," to which I replied, "I know it isn't logical, but it is still true."

## REJECTION OF THE FAMILY

As my condition worsened, my family thought that our son Lance should come home from Germany. By the time he arrived, I was at my worst. My greeting to him was, "Why did you come? I don't want you." He shot back, "For your information, I came back for Mother." He was the only one who could get me out of bed to walk around the unit. "Come and take your dancing partner with you," he said, referring to my intravenous apparatus. After two times around the unit, I headed back to the bed, despite his protests, where I stayed most of the time. I refused, unless I was forced, to bathe, to shave with the electric razor, to brush my teeth, and to comb my hair. When my family came to see me (Lucy came daily), I normally turned away from them and faced the wall by my bed. Each day, three times, a tray of food was placed by my bed in the hope that I would eat. (All the other patients went to tables to eat.) Three times a day the trays were removed untouched, often after several hours. I lost thirty pounds.

When Lance left after two weeks, I had two more delusions: 1) that he had left on the wrong day, and 2) that he was now abandoned in the airport without food or bed, forever. I thought that, as a result, his poor wife in Germany had committed suicide. I also had a delusion about our daughter Marcia, that after she had left following a visit, she had committed suicide. That night all kinds of lights went on in the unit, there were sirenlike sounds, and someone closed my door, which was unusual. I assumed all those things happened because Marcia had taken her life. When our son Dale and Bill Smith called on me the next day, I told them Marcia had killed herself. I also had a delusion that our daughter Polly in Texas was in serious difficulty. And always I was sure that none of my family, after having visited me, could ever find their cars in the parking ramp.

## PREOCCUPATION WITH DEATH

During these weeks I was preoccupied with death. I wanted to die as a way out of my psychic pain. I thought that maybe I could starve myself, but I knew that that would take a long time. When I mentioned the possibility to my psychiatrist, he said that death by starvation would be a very painful death. I recall saying to myself and others, "It is hard entering this world and it is even harder to leave."

I got a perverse satisfaction out of mentally envisioning my suicide. I did this many times a day. One thought was that if I could get out of bed with no one seeing me, lie on my back beside my bed on the floor, and place the bed wheel over my throat, I might be able to strangle myself. Even then I knew I no longer had the strength to do this. And with my door always open, there was little chance that I would not be seen.

Another—my favorite—was to fantasize that somehow I might get home for a short leave, stuff the exhaust pipe of the car in the garage, and then turn on the motor. Of course, this would have been impossible, because stuffing the exhaust pipe would have simply shut off the motor. But the minds of depressed people don't function well.

Another thought was that I would be dismissed from the hospital as an incorrigible patient, which I was. Then I would go to the banks of the Mississippi River and drown myself. The hospital was concerned enough about my being suicidal that on several occasions someone continually sat with me in my room.

Was I seriously suicidal? I would say no. I was already having a taste of hell, and death would only have given me "the full blast." Also, I believe honestly that I was afraid to try.

As indicated previously, the motion of my religious life was all downhill during my depression. Like many depressed persons, I did not "feel" the presence of God. At first in the general hospital, I tried desperately to get help for my faith. I read and reread the following Bible verses typed out for me by Bill Smith.

1.  To you, O LORD, I lift up my soul. (Psalm 25:1)

2.  The LORD is my light and my salvation;
    whom shall I fear?
    The LORD is the stronghold of my life;
    of whom shall I be afraid? . . .
    Though an army encamp against me,
    my heart shall not fear;
    though war rise up against me,
    yet I will be confident.
    One thing I asked of the LORD,
    that will I seek after;
    to live in the house of the LORD
    all the days of my life,
    to behold the beauty of the LORD,
    and to inquire in his temple. (Psalm 27:1, 3-4)

3.  I will bless the LORD at all times;
    his praise shall continually be in my mouth. . . .
    When the righteous cry for help, the LORD hears,
    and rescues them from all their troubles.
    The LORD is near to the brokenhearted,
    and saves the crushed in spirit. . . .
    The LORD redeems the life of his servants;
    none of those who take refuge in him
    will be condemned. (Psalm 34:1, 17-18, 22)

4.  Give ear to my prayer, O God;
    do not hide yourself from my supplication.
    Attend to me, and answer me;
    I am troubled in my complaint.
    I am distraught. (Psalm 55:1–2)

5.  Nevertheless I am continually with you;
        you hold my right hand.
    You guide me with your counsel,
        and afterward you will receive me with honor.
    Whom have I in heaven but you?
        And there is nothing on earth that I desire
        other than you.
    My flesh and my heart may fail, but God is the strength
        of my heart and my portion forever.
    Indeed, those who are far from you will perish;
        you put an end to those who are false to you.
    But for me it is good to be near God;
        I have made the Lord GOD my refuge,
        to tell of all your works.  (Psalm 73:23-28)

At the mental hospital, I lost all of my desire for spiritual help and believed—again, without a doubt—that I was damned to hell. My self-judgment had become so severe that I believed all of the books that I had written were shallow and nothing but dross. God's absence from my feelings had become God's judgment on me as totally evil.

I resisted all pastoral care from Bill Smith, my own pastor and even the hospital chaplain. I wanted no prayer, and once actually physically resisted a person who was attempting to exorcise the demon of depression. All of this religious alienation only increased my terror. My being alive meant that I had absolute destructive power, which I perversely enjoyed using as I fantasized about the destruction of my own family and even my daughter-in-law's parents. I also fantasized that my other daughter-in-law's parents were psychologically destroyed because of their daughter's suicide. I thought that as a result of my destructive powers, Dale and his wife, Sue, had divorced.

Another delusion, one that added to my resistance to shock treatments, was that I believed I had the power to wake up during the treatments and consciously experience the seizure. This frightened me. My other reason for resisting the treatments was that I was convinced that they would do no good. I was hopeless.

TO THE COURTROOM

Finally the day came for my court appearance. I was taken down by a sheriff's deputy—this was the first time I had left the unit—and was placed with others waiting their turn for an appearance. Some of these people, as I recall, were handcuffed. I had a court-appointed attorney with whom I was uncooperative. I refused to speak at the hearing. The court psychiatrist had interviewed me just prior to my appearance and testified to the court that I needed shock treatments. After the hearing, I asked to see the family members who were present. Then I was taken back by the sheriff's deputy to my locked unit where I headed straight for my bed.

This kind of court hearing involves two appearances. Under pressure from Lucy, the second one was speeded up. In about three days, I was taken down again. This time my delusional system was in high gear and I was sure that I would be lost forever in the anterooms of the courthouse. This time at court, my psychiatrist testified under the questioning of the county attorney for three-fourths of an hour about how badly I needed shock treatments. My attorney had a hard time defending me, pushing little things as she had to have something to say. The judge said he would render his decision within twenty-four hours.

The next morning was a Friday and the hospital staff was prepared for the shock treatment, awaiting the judge's decision. The judge ruled that I should be given shock treatments as necessary for six months at the University of Minnesota Hospital. I was sure that they would give me the treatments for the entire period and I would become a vegetable. When the time came, two security guards came to escort me—giants about 6'4" and 250 pounds. With these men before me, even in my delusional state, I knew resistance was futile. So I went on my own.

To my amazement I did not wake up during the shock treatment as I was sure I would. This put the first dent into my delusional idea of being destructively all-powerful. In fact, the shock treatment amazed me as to how simple it was. There was nothing to it. I was put to sleep and later woke up and felt nothing different. But I was still convinced that the ECT treatments would do no good. From then on I received them every other weekday.

Once again we turn to Lucy for her views on what happened during this time, particularly the court appearances.

## *Lucy's story*

Because Bill would not sign the papers agreeing to have shock treatments, we made plans to take him to court, but we first had to wait a month. During that time, Bill's depression became much worse. One evening after I came home, panic overtook me. The hospital personnel, it seemed, were doing nothing about his deteriorating condition.

I called the nurses' station and explained my panic. This nurse was not a regular, not one of the nurses whom I had come to know. I begged her to see that Bill receive water because he refused to drink fluids. She, of course, said that without a physician's order she could do nothing. She tried to calm me by saying that if there were a real danger, it would be taken care of. I hung up more panicked than ever. Somehow I felt Bill must have help.

I called again and begged her to let me talk to the intern on call. When he came to the phone, I pointed out my concern and the need for immediate action. Bill was in danger. As his wife, I knew that. I was beginning to realize that no one but I could do anything about it. Immediately the intern identified with my concern. If I was that concerned, he felt he could act. Our daughter Marcia and her husband Paul were visiting Bill that same evening when two security guards came to escort Bill to the unit for more severely disturbed patients, where intravenous and feeding tubes could be used. The next day he received them.

When I arrived the next day, a nurse who had been ministering to Bill told me how concerned she had been for him and that she was relieved that he was now being fed and given fluid. Sometimes the machine with a tube that fed Bill would fail and make horrible beeping sounds. Only some of the nurses were capable of restarting it. When I was there during one of these times, I felt very tense until we could get someone to fix it.

In his new unit everything with which Bill might conceivably commit suicide was kept from him. All doors to the rooms were left open except those of the very worst patients. The staff had to monitor the patients who were delusional to keep them from hurting each other. As I visited, I could hear the other patients talking in their various states of mind. What a place! But what if there were not such a place? Bill was safe there.

## GETTING READY FOR THE COURT APPEARANCE

When I knew we were going to court to get a decision about shock treatments for Bill, I felt that I needed to see a lawyer for power of attorney so that I would know what to do if I needed to sign papers. I was hoping to avoid this step, as I knew from Bill's own counseling experience with mentally ill students that committing anyone to treatment against his or her will could be dangerous. We had seen extreme hostility surface later against the person who signed the order. Wives would naturally not want to commit husbands. Therefore I felt the need to know more about these legal matters.

My first attempts to find a lawyer came to nothing. I was being initiated into a new area. Some of my physician friends, when I asked them, gave me names, but those lawyers turned out not to know the mental health field. Then those same lawyers did not know to whom to refer me. What I learned through all of this was that one should have a lawyer in place before one is needed. When it comes to specialists, the field of law is much more complicated than the medical field. So I made many time-consuming calls, and nothing came of them. As soon as I described my problem, the lawyers scuttled away.

Bill's rejection of help had now become total. He lay in bed all day and would not talk when the children came to see him. He initiated nothing, but we were all committed to visiting him often. Dale and Marcia came every other day. They, together with their sister in Texas, hatched a plan to have Lance come home from Germany and he did. His support was a great help. Someone was now at home with me to pick up the slack. He took over the driving, letting me out and picking me up at the hospital door that was close to the elevator. My aching leg welcomed his visit. He was also an enthusiastic cook.

By this time Bill lay or sat continually. An orderly would carry him to the tub and wash him, as every function was now being left to others. Lance was the only one who could get Bill out of bed to walk around the unit. We felt good if he made it around the unit twice.

The heartbreaking things that Bill said to me were not true, and Ted warned me that if I accepted them at face value, they would be destructive. When Ted had been depressed, he had also had delusions and knew what they could have done to his wife.

No description of Bill's illness could be adequately given on the phone. Because of this inadequacy, there were some tense moments between me and our older daughter, who lived out of state, when we talked on the phone.

Even though we had four adult children who were being very responsible and helpful, ultimately the responsibility fell to me as Bill's spouse. I had to balance the children's needs with my own. As the suspense about the treatments went on, we became more alarmed. We wondered what would happen if the treatments were denied or delayed.

## The First Court Appearance

I was headed for a new experience. The psychiatrist said we had to get Bill into court. He was losing weight rapidly, and my panic button was screaming that something had to be done before it was too late. Bill would die. The psychiatrist had repeatedly told me that the ECT would cure Bill, but now he was telling me that I would have to push for the treatments. Bill looked dreadful. He became more deranged and crazy. Besides being sure that his bowels and kidneys were no longer functioning, he was convinced that his genitals were no longer there. I pooh-poohed that, but he remained certain. I had Lance take him to the bathroom and tell his dad what he saw. When Lance assured him that everything was OK, he insisted Lance was wrong.

The time had come to go to court. Most of what the psychiatrist told me about this venture was entirely new to me. I didn't even know where the courthouse was. Since Bill could no longer make any rational decisions, the court would have to order him to have shock treatments, and by now no one doubted their necessity. The hospital social worker phoned the court and a case officer was assigned. So first I had to go to the courthouse, which was in a different county than our residence (it was in the same county as the hospital) and file for the official papers. Lance went with me, and we were taken to a private room by the case officer in the mental health division. There the forms were spread out on the table and the officer explained them. She asked us to read and sign them, which we did. We were told that there would be two court appearances, seventy-two hours apart, the first of which was to be seventy-two hours from the date of the petition. She informed us that Bill would be appointed an attorney to defend him, and after the hearing, the judge would either commit him to the treatments or not. He also had a guardian *ad litem*, a term I had never heard previously. A case officer would visit Bill first to determine if what had been planned was the correct procedure. We were told that no private attorney would be needed.

This was a very serious act, and both Lance and I were rather numb with emotion afterward. There is a great difference between talking about such an act and doing it. I told Lance and the other children that signing the document might mean the end of our marriage because sometimes when recovery does not occur, or should the court deny our petition, the patient may blame the persons who signed the document. Both of us agreed, along with other family members, that we had to take that risk.

Bill's psychiatrist also had to sign the petition as a representative of the hospital; he was taking a similar risk. On the final petition, I decided to remove Lance's name so that I alone signed the document for the family. The court appointed a "screener" who came to the hospital to interview Bill. Bill was given an injection prior to the visit so that amazingly he talked quite freely to the screener, which she reported in a document that she signed. A conference was held with the screener and the hospital staff with the decision that the court action was appropriate. A court date was set and the settlement conference was to be held immediately after the examination by the court. The court would determine a treatment plan.

When the hospital staff found out who was assigned as Bill's appointed attorney, they gasped. Not a worse person could have been found! She was an outstanding advocate of patient's rights and was known for her opposition to shock treatments. The thought that she would be defending Bill actually seemed to terrorize them. She had made a crusade of trying to prevent shock treatments from being given to anyone who refused them.

When we told Bill that he was being taken to court, his reaction was that he would not change his mind. He seemed indifferent to the whole procedure. After the screening, his attorney came to his room to talk with him, but Bill would not talk with her. After giving a few "yes" and "no" answers, he turned his back on her and faced the wall. The court-appointed guardian *ad litem*, a retired social worker, also called on Bill at the hospital. Bill wouldn't talk with him either, but I immediately perceived him to be my ally. He was older than Bill and was at least one person who agreed that Bill looked dreadful. His visit proved to him that Bill indeed needed anything that could halt the slow march toward death.

The day arrived for the court appearance. Someone had decided that Bill was well enough to be brought from the hospital. According to the court order, the sheriff had to take Bill to court despite his protests that he was too ill to go. By now he was very frail. When he arrived, he was interviewed by the court-appointed psychiatrist. Our family was seated in the audience section of the courtroom.

When Bill was brought in with his court-appointed attorney, he was a sight—a tube in his nose and his shoulder blades sticking out like angels' wings. All of us were very anxious. The outcome was so crucial and our family was so unfamiliar with how the courts operate. The hearing began with the court-appointed psychiatrist's testimony that Bill was deranged and needed ECT. Then Bill's psychiatrist from the hospital testified. Since it would be up to the hospital to prove Bill's need for the treatments, we were apprehensive at this point, having no idea of his psychiatrist's ability to do so. We were even afraid that misrepresentations and even false statements and impressions might be given. The psychiatrist turned out to be all that we could have hoped for. He spoke honestly and respectfully of Bill's case. His details were accurate and well presented. He told the court of the urgent necessity for ECT. Bill's attorney raised little resistance, but we were fearful of the next court date.

The date was then set for a week later than the required seventy-two hours. We were shocked. The postponement was due to the fact that the court psychiatrist would not be able to attend sooner.

Bill was asked if he would like to greet his family; we went to a small room together. We asked him again if he would please sign for shock treatments, but he would not. The three children and I were annoyed with him because it seemed to us that with a feeding tube in his face, he should have been able to see the need. We could not persuade him to cooperate. He treated us as though we were tricking him.

We then met in the hallway for a settlement conference— the family, social worker, psychiatrist, the assistant district attorney, and the guardian _ad litem_. I felt some action had to be taken. Perhaps what I did next was an automatic panic reaction. I shouted, "We can't wait! He must start treatments as soon as possible—this week!" The assistant district attorney said,

"Well, I see no hurry. He looks quite good for a seventy-year-old man." At that point I lost it. I raised my cane menacingly and shouted loudly, "You have to take action! You are killing him!" All who were there, including my children, were shocked, but I was quite sincere. I shouted again, "I'll take you to court for this delay if you don't act!"

Because Bill's physical condition was worsening, I wondered how much longer it would be possible to treat him. The psychiatrist was also chagrined at the delay. I knew he wished to begin the treatments that week. Finally someone asked the district attorney if the court psychiatrist's testimony could be waived. His testimony that day had very clearly been that Bill was insane and that the treatments were the only hope left. It was hard to see how any other testimony would be necessary. The court attorney said she would let us know if the date could be moved up. Soon after this, she let us know that the hearing would be in three days.

I was amused at my children's reaction to my outburst. Because it may have been the deciding factor in the decision to go ahead without the court psychiatrist's further testimony, the children finally concluded that their embarrassment was worth it. I later overheard them talking quite positively about Mom raising her cane.

## The Second Court Appearance

The next hearing three days later was a virtual repeat of the first one. We were beginning to realize the frustrations of doctors and others in practice who have to take time out to testify. We had to wait at least an hour after our scheduled time for our turn. Again the testimony of Bill's psychiatrist was given forcefully and without any reason for denial. He took all the factors into consideration. We felt very grateful to him even as we sympathized with his strain. His testimony, punctuated by the court attorney's questions, took about three-fourths of an hour. Bill's lawyer nitpicked about a procedural detail, which delayed the hearing but caused no serious problems. What a relief! Even she saw that Bill had no case against treatment. The district attorney asked Bill if he would like to say anything, and of course he demurred.

Then the next bomb fell. Instead of giving his decision then, the judge stated that he would give his decision by the next day, Friday. That was the day when the shock treatments were to have been given in the morning. If they couldn't be given then, the next opportunity would be the following Monday. That night was one of the few in which I did not sleep. I was convinced that treatment was now a life-or-death matter. Bill had been kept alive by tubes for more than two weeks. Would his mind still function?

I worried that the judge would either refuse to order treatment or that his decision would come too late for Friday's treatment. I called the children, told them we were in trouble, and asked for their support. By this time Lance had left for Germany and I was alone. The psychiatrist had told me that perhaps the call from the judge would come in time to start the treatments the next morning, but that under no circumstances could he begin without the court order.

The next morning, as soon as I thought that the hospital staff might have received some word, I called. They had heard nothing but would let me know as soon as they did hear. Never have I prayed so fervently. "Please, Lord, let the judge give the go-ahead." At 9:05, the phone rang. The judge had called in his decision: Bill was to submit to involuntary treatment. As much as could be done had been done.

## LEARNING MORE ABOUT DEPRESSION

In this section, Lucy gives her perspectives on patients' rights, hospital staff stress, and court costs.

### PATIENTS' RIGHTS

As the spouse of a mentally ill person, I would have to say that I believe there should be no rights for a mentally deranged person except those that protect that person from him or herself and others, and those that lead to healing and restoration of health. In the case of violent patients, others have the right to be protected. We have known parents battered by their mentally ill and violent children. I have much sympathy for the mentally ill, having seen a loved one in this condition, but they can be totally unable to make any rational judgments.

Families need to learn about available treatments and talk over the possibilities with the psychiatrists and others involved in the care of the depressed person (for more information on types of treatment, see pages 67-75 in chapter four). The University of Minnesota Hospital was our approved facility, and at no time did I doubt the staff's expertise and diagnosis. If the patient is willing to take medication, then normally the time should be taken to see that it works. Many times it will. The psychiatrist in Bill's case saw immediately that they could not wait for as long a time as the medication would take. Also, Bill would have refused to take the medication as he did food and liquid.

Even though Bill was obviously harming his health to a dangerous point, we had to wait for a court to make a decision for him. The expense of the delay was tremendous. The hospital and doctor bills grew. His need was so evident that all of the family would have consented to his having the electroconvulsive therapy (ECT). Even his brother who had said he had heard only bad things about ECT, but who also admitted that he really didn't know anything about them, was ready to say Bill should have them.

The media have not helped in this regard; much misleading information has been presented. In one of her programs, Oprah Winfrey interviewed several people who had had ECT. One of them persisted in describing the incident from the movie *One Flew Over the Cuckoo's Nest*. When that film was released in 1976, those scenes depicting shock treatments as punishment were already dated. That movie did much harm to the cause of mental healing. It may be true that in the past ECT was given crudely, at times as punishment, and perhaps too often. But by 1976 the improvements were in place.

After he was well, Bill was part of a local TV documentary about ECT. He spoke clearly about his healing, stating that he had no memory loss or physical impairment. He did not say that ECT would heal everybody. Another person who was interviewed on the same program told of having thirty shock treatments a number of years ago that left her with a serious memory loss. There was a strong bias in the program because the impression was given that ECT caused permanent mental damage. That was unfair because the viewers had no other source of information.

I was very fortunate having Ted as a friend who had evidence that ECT could clearly help a person and return him or her to complete normalcy. I am glad that we can now speak out to counteract the scary misinformation that flourishes.

We had seen *One Flew Over the Cuckoo's Nest* in 1976 and were influenced by the horrible scenes of ECT in that film. Perhaps it is because of impressions such as those that the law requires that the mentally ill patient sign permission to receive ECT in all cases, even when the person's health is rapidly deteriorating.

I would have given my consent immediately to ECT as Bill's depression became severe. He had just had pneumonia and needed to get back to normal health as quickly as possible. His physical problems were exacerbated by his mental illness. Only someone close to the patient can judge how rapidly he or she is going downhill and know the importance of acting quickly.

It is my conviction that Bill, in his deranged mental condition, should not have had the right to refuse to take ECT, no more than he would have had been allowed to dictate his treatment for pneumonia. As with pneumonia, time is of the essence to make recovery from mental illness possible.

## Hospital Staff Stress

The stress on the hospital staff should also have been prevented. They had to work under pressure to keep Bill as healthy as they could until they heard the court decision. Bill's feeding machine was a very delicate apparatus that often gave off odd ticking noises. It also emitted an annoying "scream" to show it was malfunctioning. The staff was subjected to this tension every day. Only one of the nurses seemed to have the expertise and patience to fix it. This high-tech machine was amazing in how it could accurately balance the foods that went into it. Yet its frequent malfunctioning was such an irritant that sometimes, in my presence, a nurse in total frustration would simply unplug it to keep it quiet. I sympathized with her. Although the hospital had technicians on call who could come, I gathered that none of them knew any more about this machine than the staff on the floor.

All of this happened in an atmosphere where many patients were potentially violent. There was a constant babble because some of the patients continually verbalized their illusions. Most of the patients showed some inappropriate behaviors and had to be monitored lest they look or go into other patients' rooms or act otherwise improperly.

## Court Costs

I need not dwell long on the expense of the court. Court costs were paid by the county and the hospital. Just the cost of the court-appointed attorney must have been quite high. These expenses could have been eliminated if there had been another way of determining that a patient should have ECT. If the panel of psychiatrists at the University of Minnesota who first examined Bill, together with the family, could have made that decision, much time and expense could have been saved. Whatever rights were being protected for Bill were certainly illusory.

# THREE

## The Miracle of Healing

THE FIRST THREE SHOCK treatments that I received did not work because I was too dehydrated. But then they became effective and I had six more. After the ninth treatment, three weeks later, the psychiatrist informed me that they were over. I also noticed that I no longer had the feeding tube in my nose. Sometime during the three weeks, when the tube had needed changing, my doctor had mercifully done that when I was "out" after one of the shock treatments. Sometime before the last treatment he had removed it altogether. I recall saying to him, "Do you mean that I am well?" He said, "Yes." And I realized then for the first time that I was well.

### MY RECOVERY, MY RESURRECTION

My experience was like an instantaneous healing, the kind with which we associate the word *miracle*. It was as though I had come from death to life, from consciously sleepless to where I could sleep. Others would tell me that I had slept, but in my conscious awareness, I thought I had not slept for two and a half months. I went from not eating to actually feeling hungry. After weeks of withdrawal from all activities on the unit, I began to participate. I recall playing Yahtzee with the recreational therapist and a couple other patients and actually enjoying it.

One reason I liken my recovery to a resurrection is because Ted had continually told me during my hospitalization that he would be going to church with me on Easter. In my depressed mind, nothing seemed more ridiculous. My last shock treatment was on Good Friday. Saturday the psychiatrist said he would let me out for a few hours to go to church if I so desired. Well, I did! As I climbed the steps of my church with my family on Easter Sunday, there was Ted waiting for me with a big smile on his face as if he were saying, "Well, I told you so, didn't I?" Each year since then we have celebrated Easter together, celebrating Jesus' resurrection, and in a small way, my own. It is interesting that I was not the only one who saw a resurrection in my recovery. A retired seminary professor greeted me on my return by calling me Lazarus.

In contrast, others saw my recovery in a more gradual way. Bill Smith recalls that I was walking around the unit prior to my last treatment, and when he arrived, I said, "Hi, Bill." Most unusual. The psychiatrist said he had noted that I had been eating some from my trays. Lucy noted that I was more rational in my speech and showed increasing activity, getting out of bed on my own and cleaning myself up. She also noticed that I was taking an interest in what she was doing. Also, I was conversing rationally about other patients in the unit.

When I was confident that I was over my depression for good, Lucy was still worried. Would I have a relapse? Would the effect of the treatments hold? And whenever I had any emotional difficulties about my health later, her fears returned. Obviously she had been somewhat traumatized by those weeks I was in the hospital.

Because my white cell count was still high, in the remaining days of my hospitalization I agreed to allow what I had refused previously: another bone marrow biopsy. The biopsy confirmed what the other had indicated, namely, that I had chronic myelomonocytic leukemia. All the time I had been depressed I regarded this as good news because I hoped it would kill me. Now that I was sane, the leukemia bothered me because it is an incurable and life-threatening disease. When I was released a week after my last treatment, I was put on Prozac for six months as a preventative against depression.

In terms of electroconvulsive therapy, where does that electric current go? It is just a small amount, the equivalent of a jolt from an electric socket. Nobody knows for sure. Yet people like myself—delusional and on the older side—find ECT eighty-five to ninety percent effective in curing depression. One psychiatrist gave me his impression that what medication does over a longer period of time, ECT does quickly. The current obviously alters the brain's chemistry where the depression is centered.

### The Return of Faith

What amazed me most after the ninth and final shock treatment was that my faith in God was back. Where is faith located, I wondered, in my brain cells? I had gone from a faith that there was a God but a God who had damned me justifiably because I was evil, to a restoration of a saving faith and a recovery of security in my salvation.

Obviously salvation cannot be dependent on what theologians call *sola fide*, faith alone. During my deepest depression I had no faith. Yet I strongly believe that had I died in my sense of damnation, I would have been saved. God had hold of me even though I had no subjective awareness of this. Salvation is by grace, *sola gratia*, through faith if one is capable of it, without faith if one is not. Grace, as gift, puts all the emphasis on God, where it had to be in my condition. As in other recoveries of what I had lost, I have never had any slipbacks in my faith. I was completely restored to my relationship with God.

It was a journey of faith also for Lucy. She had keyed into her past beliefs and depended on them to see her through. In no way did she have complete assurance that I would get well, and the experience required a reexamination of the principles of her faith also.

Though the help and support she gave me was obviously not appreciated at the time, I strongly suspect that I benefited from them. I do not know what effect she and the children's faithfulness had on me. But this I do know: in the worst of my depressed moments, I never doubted their love for me after that night of hallucination when I believed they had turned against me. Obviously they had not. But I had no love to give them and I made that obvious. I recall being concerned about being honest—if I didn't love them, I would not pretend that I did.

## *Lucy's story*

When the time came for the shock treatments, I asked if I needed to be at the hospital. Although some physicians like to have a relative present, the staff assured me that my presence was not necessary. I came as soon as I could from work. Although Bill had received his first treatment by then, I saw no change in him. I do not remember the weekend because nothing changed for Bill, but I was glad when Monday came and the treatments could continue. I was at ease now because the treatments were underway. We were finally acting on the only thing left to do.

The psychiatrist had asked for and received what is called the Price-Sheppard order, which meant that Bill became his charge for the next three months. This was a precaution because he did not know how many treatments Bill would need. Monday and Wednesday's treatments still produced no change. This was discouraging except that the psychiatrist thought Bill's dehydration might be a factor.

Then after the fourth treatment, I did notice a change. Bill was becoming more rational. His relationship skills were returning. He was willing to groom again. I made arrangements to have a barber come to the hospital to cut his hair. Bill was now more presentable. As the treatments continued, he became more sociable and conversed with many people in the ward. He says now that he was not aware of it, but his natural sociability was returning.

Finally I could tell him, "You are getting better." He was surprised to hear it.

Then the staff asked if I would like to try a home overnight visit. I was afraid of it. I didn't know if I would be able to help him if any of his symptoms returned. I was alone and if I asked anyone to come in, he would sense my uneasiness. We settled on a visit beginning in the afternoon and ending by the end of visiting hours that evening. The nurse asked me what I would cook for Bill and I decided on lentil soup because it is so nourishing. Bill's response to being home was somewhat uneasy. I sensed that he agreed with me that it would be best to return to the hospital the same day. Bill's next time home was Easter Sunday. The children were joyous to see him home. It was very touching. Five days later he was released for good. Bill was back with us!

## BILL'S RETURN TO NORMALCY

After Bill returned home, it took a while for him to become secure. Gradually, however, he began to assume his old roles. Our children were not only very supportive and joyful during this time, but actually incredulous that after such a terrible mental breakdown their father could return home and be normal. My confidence, however, was very tenuous. A physician friend had advised me that though Bill seemed to be normal, I should continue to be watchful. He had observed enough cases to know that right after treatment a patient can be suicidal even though no one is aware of it. Fortunately, I saw no such symptoms. Bill remembered his time in the hospital very well and enjoyed comparing notes with those who had been there to visit.

During his illness, Bill's brother in Ohio wanted to be of help and offered to come to Minnesota. During Bill's hospitalization, I talked frankly with him about Bill's condition and told him I really did not see a role for him at that point, so he put off the visit. But when Bill came home, I did see a role for him, called him, and he came. This turned out to be one of the most fortunate things that I did. Bill wanted to return to society and his brother facilitated that wish. He would drive him to many social events, to daily chapel at Luther Northwestern Seminary, and even to our church convention which was held there. A brother's presence was seen as natural, while a wife's presence might have been seen as suspiciously protective.

Initially I did not want Bill to go to the psychiatric unit of the hospital nor did he. It was our friend Ted Arneson, having had more than one series of ECT, who recognized his need for institutionalization. I personally was afraid of mental hospitals and psychiatrists.

The court appearance was traumatic for the family. Those who were working had to take the entire day off because there was no way of knowing precisely when the case would come up. We had to accept the testimony of the psychiatrist who knew Bill only in his illness and not as his family did. I doubt that every patient is fortunate enough to have such a gifted, careful, and accurate communicator as Bill's psychiatrist turned out to be. What if the case had not been as clear cut as Bill's and the sharp court-appointed attorney had been more convincing? What if the judge's decision had been "no"?

I was told by the hospital that if I as spouse did not take Bill to court, the hospital would have to do it. This would have delayed the court appearance even further and Bill probably would have died in the meantime. So, needless to say, we are grateful for all who played a role, large or small, in Bill's dramatic recovery.

## Bill speaks:

Three professional people who were with me during my hospitalization gave me their observations of me: Dr. Robert Howe, hematologist; Pam Krieder, registered nurse; and Dr. William Sheehan, psychiatrist.

### Dr. Robert Howe, hematologist

Dr. Howe called on me several times because of the diagnosis of leukemia, although I did not know the reason for his visits at the time. Dr. Howe described me as a vegetable.

Dr. Howe: "You sat on your bed with your head down. There was no spontaneity, no expression on your face. You contributed nothing although you would answer my questions."

*Pam Kreider, registered nurse*

Nurse Pam Kreider could get me to do things that others could not. There was a firmness in her voice that even in my depression I recognized. After getting the necessary permission, she turned over her chart notes to me:

*3/10* Patient states his kidneys are failing and there is no bowel peristalsis. He states, "It does no good to talk about it."

*3/11* Continues to state concern about kidney failure and lack of peristalsis. When asked if he wants to die, he replied, "I'm doing that slowly. I have no choice in the matter. I'll eat and drink to prove to you that what I am saying is true. I may require bowel surgery for an impaction. A while back I woke up and knew everything was different now. It's no use talking about it. You people don't care. You're here for the money." Patient is refusing medications and states he doesn't want his wife to visit. Appears severely depressed and is convinced he is dying. Yet states he will be in the hospital "for the next twenty years."

*3/16* Patient refused breakfast. Required a firm approach, but allowed patient to choose what time he would bathe. Stated he couldn't move right arm but did so when encouraged. "What's the use," he said. "Now we have a big problem here; now I'm urinating too much." Patient was reassured that this was not so, but he insisted.

*3/17* Patient more withdrawn. Refuses all food and fluids. Brightened during visit from family, then returned to withdrawn state. Refused to wash, was not given an option and so staff washed him. Advised he needed to get up and walk, and was then assisted by two staff. States, "What's the use."

*3/19* Elbow is swelling and patient states, "It got better on its own before. I can't go home again."

*3/23* He states sense of sight and hearing will leave him. Refused hygiene. Staff assisted. Insisted he did not need to void, but when taken to the bathroom, he did urinate.

*3/25* Refuses all oral intake. Requires physical prompting to turn self in bed, otherwise lays still. Pleaded with me to stop the tube feeding, stating his kidneys have shut down and "it will all come flooding out."

*3/29* Continues to refuse food/fluid. More resistant to self-care. Expresses fear of losing hearing and sight.

*4/3* After five ECTs. Affect more spontaneous, taking fluids by mouth, seems to have an interest in environment.

*4/6* Eating well. Stated depression had lifted after ECT today, but that it is back, "Now that I have lived through the day." Continues to believe kidney and bowel function will cease. Believes he needs surgery for this. Expresses concern that a bowel obstruction will develop. Was reassured we can give him something for his bowels. He replied, "Oh yeah, what? Dynamite!"

*4/8* Brighter, dramatic improvement in both affect and mood. Attending to self-care without prompting. Spontaneous conversation.

*4/16* Affect bright. States bowel status is "just right."

*4/18* Bright and independent. Voices no concern about physical problems.

*Dr. William Sheehan, psychiatrist*

Psychiatrist William Sheehan was the resident that was assigned to my care. He was outstanding in every way. The following are his observations:

*March 11.* Took up my assignment on the Red Team; my predecessor informed me that the gaunt and disheveled man to whom she introduced me was a scholar who had written a score of books and was an authority on the book of Job. He might have been Job himself—the comparison would often suggest itself to me in ensuing weeks.

This was a man who had been sick hardly a day in his life—who still ran four miles several times a week, and swam on alternate days. Though now seventy, he had been used to being in control, to being on top of his form, intellectually and physically. He looked younger than his seventy years. He had had a premonition while in the hospital for pneumonia of approaching death. When he was told he had leukemia, it was a discovery which to his mind confirmed that his dark premonition had come true; his will—his ability to fight the disease—collapsed. By the time I met him, he had lapsed into depression.

In his own mind he was doomed, as certain as he had been of anything in his life that his was a posthumous existence now, and that any efforts of mine or anyone else's were futile. He was at the center of the deepest hell and concentrated in himself all the evil of the universe. At first he agreed to start the medication I prescribed for him, if only to humor me. Soon he changed his mind, and stubbornly refused; he was convinced it would be of no use. For the same reason he gave up eating. It was clear that we would be unable to wait for the leisurely course of medications to take effect, and I had to take up the cudgel on behalf of ECT. I remember trying to persuade him that the treatments would likely be effective, but it was far from easy to make such a case, given his resistance and conviction that this treatment or any other would be to no avail. I was not entirely surprised when he continued to resist my efforts at persuasion. Nevertheless I persisted—seconded by his family, whose doubts about what I was proposing were more easily overcome. At last he weakened. I felt a sense of triumph—qualified, however, by my own concern that the treatment that I was advocating might, after all, prove less effective than I hoped, but in any case my triumph was short lived. The day of the first treatment he again changed his mind.

His family was unable to understand how someone in his condition could be allowed to decide something for himself. His friend, who had referred him for treatment, attempted to persuade and finally to drag him into the ECT suite against his will. I was flustered and disappointed, and I left the ward feeling defeated.

I knew from previous experience that it would do no good to try to use rational arguments to persuade someone in his condition. His sense of alienation from God and family was absolute. There was something almost grandiose in his despair. He stopped drinking now as well as eating, and we had to begin giving him IV infusions. At least he cooperated with those, and didn't pull the line out as I'd feared he might (his veins were fragile already). We were backed into a corner now—there was no choice but to go to court and get the order we needed to impose (inflict) ECT on him, that effective (but only too medieval-looking) method of treatment. With a sense of desperation I knew that it had to be done, but it was wrenching to have to testify against my own patient and force him to accept these treatments or any others against his will. He sat sullen and silent in the courtroom. I could only imagine what thoughts were going through his mind. I knew the order would be forthcoming, and it was. The first shock treatment resulted in an ineffectually short seizure, but the rest went smoothly—there were nine as I recall. Before we were through we had to give up on the IV route because we could no longer access a vein, and we put an NG tube down his nose to keep him hydrated and nourished. After a few days it became disengaged and we had to put in a second, but I decided to put this one in when he was under general anesthesia before his next treatment. Despite blandishments of the nursing staff—and the inconvenience of the NG tube—he still refused to eat. He had received countless cards from well wishers but took no interest in any of them, and turned away old friends who came to visit.

Finally—the turning point, as it turned out—he agreed to eat. We pulled the NG tube and hoped; he did begin to eat on his own. Each day he seemed to grow a little stronger. By now six weeks had passed; both of us had struggled with each other, almost like adversaries—although it was his depression, not him, that I was pitted against. A formidable adversary indeed! He had come into the hospital at the end of February; it was now April, and spring, close to Easter. It was a fitting time for his spirits to reawaken. I'm not sure how I knew it—one of those intuitions on which a clinician relies—but I realized that he had had his last shock treatment. As the birds made melody outside his window, his depression had been mastered—it had spent its raging force, the storm of the brain had passed, and he began to emerge from hell.

# LEARNING MORE ABOUT DEPRESSION

In this section we will discuss the ways depression can affect people at different ages as well as factors that predispose people toward depression. We will look at how depression can affect children and youth, people at mid-life, and the elderly.

## CHILDREN AND YOUTH

Research has shown that children are often more depressed than we realize. Our culture lays heavy demands on everyone, even on children, for establishing self-worth. At the same time it is effective in dashing people's hopes for achieving this worth.

Our culture provides little or no mechanism for rewarding our contributions just as they are. Instead, the emphasis is placed on continually getting or doing more. Good parents are those who keep encouraging their children to try harder and to go further. Rarely do we take time with a child just to show approval and satisfaction. Nurturing adults need to affirm children. A child who is so nourished becomes a nurturing adult who accepts and nourishes children.

Parents who feel beaten down by our culture are not usually in a position to give their children what they need, namely, the kind of love and acceptance that will help them feel good about themselves. In school they may not receive affirmation if they do not do well, and they are not likely to do well if they are depressed over their self-worth.

Studies show that through the first eight years of schooling, female students do not receive the attention or rewards—even from their female teachers—that their male counterparts do. Males in our society tend to be seen as more promising and more productive than females, and perhaps just more important. It is good that empirical studies have revealed this discrepancy to us. Girls treated in such a manner can feel angry and depressed, especially when they see that nothing is reversing this trend and they continue to be unrewarded as the years go by. The influence of the home can be the key to reversing this trend by giving equal value to girls and expecting equal responsibility of the boys. The schools may be simply reinforcing an attitude in our society that is so ingrained that it is not perceived until comprehensive testing brings it to light.

In their teen years, children may begin to show their depression through bizarre and even violent behavior. Often there is far more depression than is generally recognized. Our son Dale, who has worked with youth for many years, wrote a book entitled *Way Down: A Look at Teenage Depression* (Minneapolis: Augsburg, 1984), in which he describes several symptoms of depression as trees that hide the forest. Doing poorly at school, where before the youth was doing well, can be a symptom of depression. Other symptoms are becoming truant, becoming delinquent in behavior, and hanging out with bad company when before the young person had wholesome friends.

As Dale pointed out, these deviant behaviors are due to the fact that the teenagers usually do not recognize their own feelings—in this case, depressed feelings. Their destructive behavior is their way of trying to cope with their feelings. The anger that is often a symptom of depression is usually more pronounced in teenage depression. The anger shown by violent youth groups could well be due to depression. For those youth, often inner-city and minority, their future seems to them to be dim or even hopeless. We might be wise to view the rising violence among such youth as symptoms of their depression. It is no wonder that with the increase of these destructive behaviors among our youth, the suicide rate is increasing alarmingly.

In our city, a youth was arrested and convicted of deliberately shooting a policeman while he was drinking coffee in a restaurant. The youth's mother gave her lament to a reporter. Her son, she said, didn't see any hope for himself in the future. So in a desperate attempt to find some meaning for his life, he was drawn to a gang of youth of like-minded negativity. Banded together, they experienced power. "I knew what was happening to him," the mother lamented, "but I felt powerless to stop it— and now look what's happened!"

Inner-city youth often see no meaning for their lives and no chance or purpose in their future. They turn to gangs as a palliator for their pain, which is depression, but they neither recognize it nor know how to handle it. Gangs, to them, may seem to be one way to reduce their distress.

## PEOPLE AT MID-LIFE

Depression can occur in mid-life for many reasons and in many situations. For men, the workplace is usually a troublesome area. However, as situations change, this is becoming increasingly true for women as well. A person may experience a vocational crisis and his or her sense of calling may seem to be collapsing under the weight of disappointments. Such difficulties are more likely in times of economic recession when lack of job security and layoffs are traumatic for many people.

Problems at work can be a source of depression. A new boss may be "the Pharaoh who knew not Joseph" and may not be as receptive or friendly toward an employee as the previous boss. One may be experiencing frustrations in one's career, and future advancements. And in a society where so much emphasis is placed on occupation, these frustrations may seem extremely threatening. A person may begin to dislike going to work, finding it difficult to get up in the morning. When this occurs, the person is already depressed. When such depressed thinking takes over, the person sees the future as no longer large enough to contain hope. As the depression worsens, there seems to be no way he or she can make it. Of course, none of these conclusions is rational, but the depressed mind is anything but rational.

The same kind of depressing thoughts can occur over a collapsing marriage or over children whose behavior is not all that one had hoped for. Mid-life is a time when marital and family problems are most likely to occur. Because of their orientation to the home, women have been most likely to be hit by depression in these areas. But times are changing; men are now becoming more home oriented. The result of the disappointments and disillusions is that the depressed mind thinks, "I am a failure, a disappointment to all whose respect I had wanted."

The symptoms of depression in mid-life are the changes in one's normal behavior, such as loss of appetite, difficulty sleeping, and loss of interest in sex. Usually a depressed person becomes more quiet, rarely smiles, and has little spontaneity. Often he or she loses interest in work or home duties and just goes through the motions. Among professional people, the end product of such depression, if it is not treated, is labeled with the euphemisms "burn out" or "nervous breakdown." These terms simply mean that in their depression they have reached a place where they are no longer able to function in their duties or obligations.

In mid-life a woman may be quite vulnerable to depression for a number of reasons. Her children have probably reached adolescence, and new skills have to be learned to deal with this troublesome time. It can be a humbling experience. Also at this time, some of her dreams for her children and marriage threaten not to be realized. Few are the children or husbands who can fulfill all expectations. As she works on her own interests and concerns, she may feel a sense of failure. If a woman has a job outside the home and has a sense of achievement there, her negative feelings about herself, her family, her home, and her other concerns can be counteracted to some extent. A woman's family members and friends need to watch for symptoms of depression and urge her to get help as needed.

Menopause is often a wake-up call for a woman to become a more authentic person. Physical changes must be accepted, but they can be an occasion for a new emphasis on personal growth. By using the intellectual discipline she has gained by experience, a woman can respond to her spirituality and learn to be an even more authentic person in line with her gifts and calling. If she does so, she has true power of authority. The depression of a woman in mid-life is often a compounding of derogatory comparison and confusion in finding her true self (more about women and depression can be found on pages 92-94).

But those coming changes in a woman's body, as unwelcome as they may be, may not be as stressful as the challenges of living with various disappointments in her life to this point. Lack of satisfaction in any area easily transfers to another. What both women and men fear at this time are the two words "too late."

Family members, siblings, and parents can support a woman in mid-life depression. She will seek their approval and be very sensitive about their reactions. Church groups can help the woman apply the gospel to her life. Older women, who have a mission as part of the body of Christ, and have been through this period themselves can gently affirm the mid-life woman in her despair. Whatever the problem, it is not permanent. The joy of God's help plays an important role in lifting the depression.

Men are most susceptible to depression in mid-life when they become alarmed over the aging process or are unhappy in their work. Because physical fitness is important to many men, they watch signs of decline with dismay. In our culture, for many men, their worth centers on their work. Failure there, or fear of failure, can be frightening. In our day of frequent changes in a company's management, a man's future can quickly be turned around. So men are challenged in mid-life to find measurements for their worth other than their work and to come to terms with their mortality.

Friends, relatives, and even family members who are at least somewhat freed up from the hold of our culture's values and priorities can offer invaluable help to both men and women. They can help them to learn to reframe their outlook and affirm a positive attitude.

Education in these areas of trouble in mid-life can also be helpful in avoiding depression. Community education classes, seminars, retreats, courses in colleges and universities, adult forums, and classes in church are often available. Instruction in its various forms can explain what before were riddles. Men and women who understand themselves and what is going on in their lives can often stave off any mid-life depression. Many men and women return to school and achieve success and self-esteem. Both men and women can also turn to the more spiritual side of life during this time and find in the teachings of the Christian faith much help both in preventing depression and in giving the insights needed to help it lift.

## PEOPLE IN THEIR LATER YEARS

Because of the nature of aging, and particularly the attitudes toward aging in our anti-aging culture, older people have a high rate of depression. People over sixty are more likely to suffer from depression than any other age group, and they are the least likely to acknowledge their depression. Three percent of Americans over sixty-five are chronically depressed. Among residents of nursing homes and care centers, seven to twelve percent suffer from mild forms of depression, and twenty to forty percent of those residents are very depressed. Older people can develop cognitive problems due to their depression and then mistakenly assume they have Alzheimer's disease. Sometimes the depression may be caused by some of the medications older people take ("Depression in Elderly: Attitudes Die Hard," Minneapolis: *Star Tribune*, February 27, 1994, page 3E).

The longer people live, the more losses they experience. This pileup of losses can be depressing. They lose loved ones, their jobs, perhaps their homes, and some of their abilities (for example, singing or carpentry). Often they experience the loss or reduction of healthy body functioning (walking, seeing, hearing). Increasing health problems can add to their unhappiness and restrict the lifestyle that prevents depression. Our culture inhibits older people from grieving their losses in healthy ways. In our society, we tend to discourage them from talking about their grief over their losses or problems, even though we may allow a short period of tolerance. Then they are supposed to "get over it."

But most important, our culture in its ageist discrimination undermines the value of the elderly. They are old, retired, and "out of it." This cultural judgment is difficult to adjust to positively. Aging, as far as our culture is concerned, is an end and not a beginning of a new and challenging stage of life. When older people internalize this attitude, which is easy to do, it can easily lead to depression.

Older people may see their future as bleak and may wish to die. The elderly often show their depression by not talking much. They sit quietly in group conversation. In contrast to youth, they rarely show anger in their depression because they can easily see that it is not acceptable for older people to show anger. Since as they age they grow increasingly dependent on others, they cannot afford to alienate themselves. Older people frequently stuff their anger in their depression. There are some exceptions, of course, and some whose anger is on the surface are difficult to care for. Often they are "punished" by their significant others by reduced care, less frequent contacts, or perhaps no contact at all.

In their chronic depression in which the future is bleak, older people may recall the past in negative ways because they are influenced by their depressive perspective. They may look back on their life as a series of blunders, mistakes, and tragic times. On the other hand, for some the past can become so unrealistically positive, based largely on denial, that the present has no way to compete with it. Yet for most depressed elderly, the past is seen as a series of losses and disappointments, irreparable as far as they are concerned.

Men's identification with their work for their worth comes to a crashing halt with retirement. What then can a man do that can provide him with a sense of worth? Too many men die shortly after retirement because they are not able to find an answer to that question.

One man told me the story of his father and his uncle. Both retired the same year. His father had no hobbies. His work was his life. He was lost in retirement and died within a year. His uncle had many hobbies and went to work on them immediately. Some of them had a monetary value and soon he was selling his products. Before long he had a business built up that occupied most of his time. He is still living at ninety-four. The difficulty men have in our culture finding meaning beyond retirement may account, at least in part, for the fact that so many more women than men live into their late senior years. Obviously we have a challenge here to help retired men find a new and more realistic orientation for their worth.

The ultimate path to one's worth is the Christian gospel which offers the good news that comes from Christ and assures us of our worth. The church has a critical role to play in helping people of all ages know God's unconditional love for them and in helping them find positive ways to prevent depression.

# FOUR

## *Continuing Recovery*

WHILE HEALED COMPLETELY FROM my clinical depression, I was still vulnerable because of my physical health problems. By no means was I out of the woods. Dealing with a life-threatening illness, chronic leukemia, for which there is no cure, was a new experience for me. It takes some time to adjust. I explained to Lucy on several occasions that I was having difficulty coming to terms with the diagnosis. Visualizing my death in the not-too-distant future unfortunately was a realistic picture. Of course, Lucy was troubled by the news about my leukemia as well and would try to comfort me by reminding me that she too was vulnerable, that none of us knows when death will strike. While recognizing the truth of this, somehow it did not remove me from being a "special case." After all, I knew my diagnosis and the prognosis from the medical field.

When in social gatherings, my being a "special case" would hit me even harder and I would envision myself in a coffin with these people gathered around viewing me. But through it all, I had no depression. Perhaps that was the real miracle. I suppose knowing that I had a life-threatening disease helped me also. Just the thought of seeing myself dead seemed to give me courage to say and do what previously I would have backed away from. The thought seemed to give me authority or permission to do what previously might have been difficult.

# The Return to Activities

By fall I had returned to part-time teaching at Luther Northwestern Seminary. I had retired that spring, having reached the mandatory age of seventy, but when our president pointed out that I had not taught more than half of my last year and asked me if I would like to replaced a fellow teacher in our department who was taking a sabbatical, I accepted.

Along with Lucy, I also conducted a workshop on depression that same fall that went well and seemed to have no adverse effects on me. I began accepting speaking engagements and resuming my normal lifestyle as best I could.

In late summer Lucy had decided it was time for her to have a hip replacement. Those close to me were concerned about me during this time. Lucy arranged for a friend to stay with me while she had her surgery and for our daughter Marcia to stay with me evenings while Lucy recovered in the hospital.

Bill Smith continued to minister to me as my pastoral counselor. It was believed that my high white cell count was causing me joint problems. During one of his visits with me when I was quite laid up with gout, Bill looked anxiously at me and said, "You're not depressed?" "No," I said. "Not depressed at all, but I am discouraged." Bill replied, "I'm so relieved." He knew that I knew the difference.

## Ménière's Disease

But then came the one problem too many. Ten months after I left the hospital I woke up during the night feeling very dizzy. In reaching for the closet door to steady myself and discovering it was open, I fell hard onto the closet floor. I called to Lucy and she helped me back into bed.

After much doctoring, it was determined that I had Ménière's disease, a disease of the inner ear that is incurable, but not life-threatening. It was miserable being dizzy all the time. In addition, there was a loss of hearing in my left ear. For a short time I used a walker. The constant dizziness except when lying down began to get to me.

One day I felt a frightening feeling that I had not had since the hospital—depression. In contrast to my clinical depression, this was different—a situational depression (as described in chapter one). The situation, of course, was the constant vertigo which I began to hate.

Whether a negative situation like mine leads to depression or not depends on how much stake the person has in a different outcome. When the stake is high, then often times the roof can cave in. In my case, I could have endured a siege of vertigo without depression. However, when the medications did not work and I knew that the condition was incurable, depression began to hit me.

## Learning Cognitive Behavioral Therapy (CBT)

The fear of depression sent me into immediate action. I attended a meeting where Dr. Paula Clayton of the University of Minnesota Department of Psychiatry was also in attendance. I told her of my situation and asked her for the name of the best cognitive behavioral therapist in the area. She gave me a recommendation. I also remember telling her that I was still beginning each day by saying, "This is the day which the Lord has made and I will rejoice and be glad in it," even though I didn't feel that way anymore.

I made an appointment with the therapist she had mentioned. I was prepared to go back for outpatient shock treatments and rather expected the therapist to recommend them. But after interviewing me, he said that he had known of my previous depression, being on the psychiatric staff, and this was not that kind of depression. "We can handle this with cognitive behavioral therapy," he said, "but it will take six weeks before you should expect improvement."

He immediately put me back on Prozac and then began three months of coaching me on the principles of CBT. In my observation, CBT is the counseling method most successful in dealing with situational depression (see pages 69-70 for more information).

This was labeled a mild depression by the therapist. It is one that most people who have been depressed or who are depressed can identify with much easier than they can with my clinical depression. This situational depression was much different in many ways from my clinical depression. I had no premonition about not recovering. I put all my energies into getting well. I was determined to beat this depression as fast as I could.

Remembering me from my hospitalization, the therapist said during our sessions that he had heard that I had written some books. I said that I had and then he asked how many. When I said thirty, I don't think he ever completely recovered.

Though I was miserable, I was able to continue my daily obligations, and although difficult, I believe I did them fairly well. That was something I had been unable to do during my clinical depression. During my situational depression, doing my activities was part of my therapy. As part of the behavioral emphasis of CBT, my therapist encouraged me to do more than teach a course a quarter. "Go out and get a job, even if you don't get paid." I contacted Lutheran Social Service and was hired as a part-time pastoral counselor. So I was counseling and teaching while I was depressed and, to my knowledge, no one except Lucy, my therapist, and my pastoral counselor knew about my situational depression.

Because Bill Smith was preoccupied with his own problems at the time and I needed a pastoral counselor, I asked Mel Kimble, another colleague, to serve that role. Of course, Lucy was very worried about me, but she saw how determined I was this time to get help and to do everything I could to get well, and so she encouraged me in my CBT.

It is this kind of determination to go through the motions of my day's obligations whether I felt like it or not that was the key to overcoming my situational depression. There were times when I lost myself in my teaching or counseling and forgot that I was depressed. Of course, the awareness returned soon enough. I didn't want to be dizzy and was resisting having to live this way. I suppose in my subconscious I was saying, "God, you gave me a clinical depression and chronic leukemia, and now you throw this at me. It's a bit much." My healing came as a surrender to my condition—an acceptance of it as a lifetime affliction.

Having been a counselor for many years, I was now on the receiving end. I looked forward to going to my counseling, and when there, I kept hoping the time would not be up. How dispirited I felt when the therapist would say, "Well, that's it for today. I have other engagements that I must get to." I alarmed him once when I told him how much it meant to me to talk with him. "Listen," he said, "I'm a coach. You're the one that has to do it." He could see my growing dependency on him and the counseling sessions and tried to discourage it. All of this, of course, helped me understand my own counselees better and to appreciate where they were.

Lucy saw gradual improvement during my sessions with CBT. My therapist also saw this gradual improvement. However, I did not. In fact, I was worried that the therapist might give up on me because I was not making progress. Yet once again for me, the depression lifted almost instantaneously. I finally experienced totally what my therapist had been drilling into me cognitively, namely that being dizzy, as miserable as it is, did not have to mean being depressed. I see now that part of my depression was due to the fact that I was angry over being dizzy and refused to accept it. However, I never verbalized this and perhaps was not even consciously aware of it. Depression became my way of showing this anger and resistance.

I continued to have physical problems, including a broken ankle. About three-fourths of the way through my situational depression, I was getting out of bed, and I suppose, due to my dizziness, I lost my balance, fell, and my ankle pushed hard against the bedroom door. X rays showed a break. My orthopedic physician, whom I had known for years, said, as he put on my cast and told me it would need to stay on six weeks, that he had never seen me look so down. To me, it seemed that the one thing I didn't need just then in my vulnerability was a broken ankle. The broken ankle was also an added burden for Lucy. For six weeks she had to drive me wherever I had to go. She encouraged me to get some form of exercise. Because both walking and swimming were out, I found the answer in my stationary bicycle, which I discovered I could ride with the cast.

## LEARNING MORE ABOUT DEPRESSION

After hearing my story, you may wonder if there are any positive benefits of depression. Depression does no one any good. It only complicates further whatever situations, disappointments, and problems that one has found depressing. So I believe we need to go all-out to avoid or head off depression in ourselves and others. But by the same token, in depression we have entered into the borderland of hell. When we recover—God grant that we all do—life becomes much more like the borderland of heaven.

After depression one has new life. One experiences life as never before. I have had great happiness in living since my depressions and I believe the awful contrast between the two at least partially accounts for this. Life after depression is analogous to the idea of resurrection, and this resurrection is to a new life, not the old one. The values I believed in, those that go with my Christian faith, now came front and center. I know now, in a way never before experienced to this extent, that this is all there really is. Priorities are much easier to follow now.

As he was dying, Lee Atwater, former GOP national chair, said that putting God first was the only solution to our nation's many problems. The approach of death was for him like the lifting of depression was for me in bringing a clarity of vision rarely found otherwise.

Since 1915, the risk of depression has increased worldwide, nearly doubling for each successive generation. It is also happening with younger people, and the gap between men and women is narrowing. Women have tended to have more depression than men, but the risk of depression for young men is now rising to the levels for women (Norman Brown, "Defeating Depression," *Northwest Airlines World Traveler*, #3, 1994, page 68).

Depression is the most curable of mental illnesses, yet it accounts for most of our suicides. Fifteen percent of those who are depressed kill themselves. These are preventable deaths; therefore all efforts should be made to make treatment available to depressed people. Ted Arneson, who sits on many boards in the state of Minnesota including the Governor's Committee on Mental Illness, has made it his goal to cut the number of suicides due to depression in half in this state during his lifetime.

Depression will usually lift by itself without treatment after a period of time, maybe one year, two years, or three years. This is particularly true for young people. However, I am aware of an older man who has been depressed for three and a half years. It is best not to wait for recovery without doing anything, because in the meantime much harm can be done to one's health, career, marriage, family, and relationships.

But what do we do? In order to respond helpfully when we or others experience depression, we need to know something about the many treatments that are available. This section will summarize some of the main ones.

## TREATMENTS AND THERAPY

### Medication

The big breakthrough in the treatment of depression came in the 1950s with the use of medications. These medications affect the brain's chemistry in a way that can alleviate depression. There are at least eighteen major kinds of antidepressants; they are available only by prescription. One that is currently used often is Prozac. A physician may have to change the depressed person's medication or readjust the dosage to achieve the needed help, and that process may take time. If a medication is not helping after the predicted time, it should be changed. Because of the variety of these medications and the possible need for adjustment, it is wise to go to a specialist, namely a psychiatrist who works with mood disorders. Other medical doctors can prescribe them, but they are the specialty of the psychiatrist.

The problem with antidepressants, particularly in the past, has been the side effects. For some people, the drugs seem to slow the brain's functioning or leave them feeling woozy. This was true in Ted's depression, and he came to the conclusion that the medication was only adding to his depression. He was a busy executive, running his own company, and he had to keep mentally sharp to remain in competition. He wasn't able to do it. His psychiatrist gave him another medication that worked much better for him.

The big advantage of the drug Prozac is that for most people it has no side effects. I have taken it on two occasions and experienced no side effects at all. I don't believe that medication should be used by itself for depression, but rather it should be accompanied by psychotherapy, perhaps cognitive behavioral therapy or other therapies, including pastoral counseling. By the same token, I believe that the verbal therapies should be accompanied by medication to treat the depression. Medication is given for all kinds of depression because one never knows if and how much of the depression is due to physiological factors. This needs to be considered, not only for clinical and chronic depressions, but also for longer-lasting situational depressions.

Because sleeping is a problem for many depressed persons, sleeping medications may also be prescribed. During my clinical depression, the hospital gave me Halcyon. I took it even though I had previously heard from a friend how this drug had caused him all kinds of emotional problems. The effect of Halcyon for me lasted only about two hours and gave me only a fitful sleep during this time. Finally it had no effect on me and I took no medication for my sleeping problems the last two months of my hospitalization.

In my situational depression, I again had trouble sleeping. This time at my therapist's suggestion, I took Ativan. For me this was the ideal sleeping pill. It gave me a good, restful sleep and kept me asleep all night. I was not sleep deprived, which may have hastened my recovery. Ativan can have side effects, but I did not experience them.

## Cognitive Behavioral Therapy (CBT)

Cognitive behavioral therapy (CBT) is widely used in the treatment of depression. It is called cognitive because it focuses on thought. This is based on the fact that one cannot control one's feelings in depression, but one can control one's thoughts. Thoughts are the progenitors of feelings.

I say "fact" because of my own experience as a client in CBT. I discovered that it works. I could control my thoughts, although it was very difficult and I needed to be persistent. There is a time lag before the feelings catch up to the thoughts, and that is where persistence is needed.

So, by the principles of CBT, when people are feeling depressed, they trace the thought that is causing the feelings and challenge the thought for its rationality. For example, one typical thought is that the person thinks that he or she will never get over the depression. Is this a rational thought? Obviously not, because the person would have to be God to know the future with such certainty. So the person evicts this depressed thought and puts a rational thought in its place. "I don't know the future but I hope I will get well."

Depressing thoughts continue to return, but each time the person has the power to go through the above procedure again and again. The big problem is discouragement in not seeing immediate results in the face of the necessity to keep up the procedure. I found St. Paul's words very helpful in resisting discouragement: "Let us not grow weary in well-doing, for in due season we shall reap, if we do not lose heart" (Galatians 6:9, RSV). I believed that this continual control of my thoughts was my "well-doing."

The behavioral side of CBT stresses the depressed person's need to keep actively involved in life. This means that if one is working, one should keep on working if one can. It also means adding activities to the normal schedule, such as social activities and volunteer work. These strategies, of course, help the depressed person fight the tendency to withdraw, which would only accelerate the depression.

*Interpersonal and Psychodynamic Therapies*

Other therapies helpful in depression are interpersonal therapy and psychodynamic therapy. Interpersonal therapy focuses on one's current and past relationships that may be aggravating the depression. Psychodynamic therapy focuses on one's past experiences that may not have been happily resolved and that consequently may be contributing to the depression. It also focuses on the significant current reality in the depressed person's life.

Some people may find it helpful to deal with the subconscious, and that is something CBT does not do. Here other therapies are useful. After I had finished my CBT and my depression was over, I still felt the need to get help in looking at my total self. I arranged to have three sessions with an interpersonal therapist where this need was met. I believe that for me this additional therapy helped seal the end of my depression.

Some depressed people need to work on their long-repressed or bypassed anger as part of the healing of their depression. A former student of mine who was depressed, a young woman in her twenties, was hospitalized after a suicide attempt. She received two sets of shock treatments but they did not help her. What did help was a cathartic therapy in which the therapist kept with her until the "dam" broke. As she explained to me later, "I even banged my head on the table—it came out so fiercely. I couldn't believe I had that much stuffed within me." Having such repressed negative feelings, including anger, is sometimes the result of a person having had good but oppressive parents who were "always right." Guilt over having anger, even hate, toward such "good" parents can cause severe repression of anger. As a backlash, a depression may subsequently emerge.

## Pastoral Counseling

Another verbal therapy for depressed persons is my own area of expertise, pastoral counseling. Pastoral counseling can easily incorporate several of the other therapeutic emphases just described into its own uniqueness. For instance, the principles of CBT, using a scriptural basis, can easily be incorporated into pastoral counseling. I have taught my pastoral counseling students to make use of the strengths of other therapies.

Pastoral counseling has the advantage of having the symbol of the presence of God in its ministry. In the language of systems counseling, which emphasizes that all of our significant relationships are joined together by systems or channels that highly influence us in our development as individuals, pastoral counseling is structured to focus on the divine system, our relationship with God.

This divine system also is highly influential with us as individuals. The pastor's presence, as well as his or her prayers and use of Scripture, can be extremely helpful to the depressed person. Before my depression moved me beyond his help, Bill Smith's presence, prayers, and use of Scriptures were most helpful to me. I looked forward to his visits and hated to see him leave. He wrote out helpful Bible passages on a sheet of paper at each visit, went over them with me, and then left them for me to consider. (Some of them are printed on pages 29-30 in chapter two.) I still use them on occasion.

After my condition degenerated into a serious clinical depression, Bill Smith's presence was one of the few still allowed. Although I did not appreciate that presence at the time and told him so and asked him not to return, he did return again and again. Now in retrospect, I believe his presence was helpful even then and I deeply appreciate his giving it to me.

Prayer itself is an antidepressant. Pastoral prayers, because of who is praying them, have added significance. Henri Nouwen, in his book *The Road to Daybreak* (New York: Doubleday, 1988, page 119), tells how a friend's depression was relieved by someone praying for him. "The depression lessened after her prayer. . . . it was her agonizing prayer which brought all of his feelings of humiliation, rejection and resentment before God that took his inner darkness away." Speaking of himself, Nouwen says, "So little is needed to slip me into a depression. I am amazed by the fragility of my emotional balance. The only thing I can do is look at my emotional state with a certain distance and realize how easily everything turns dark. It is only a truly God-centered life that will pull me out of depression and give me hope" (pages 166-67). It is this God-centered life that pastoral counseling is uniquely fitted to facilitate.

The Scriptures, particularly the Psalms, bear out Nouwen's observation about prayer. Psalm 88 is perhaps the most poignant example. The author is obviously a depressed person. From beginning to end, he expresses his deep feelings of agony. But throughout the psalm, his words are an experience of prayer. The psalm is dialogical, the exercise of the divine system. This is in contrast to introspection, which for depressed people is an unhealthy exercise.

> Thou hast put me in the depths of the Pit,
> in the regions dark and deep.
> Thy wrath lies heavy upon me,
> and thou dost overwhelm me with all thy waves.
> (Psalm 88:6-7, RSV)

The last verses are more personal in the psalmist's relationship with God, although the thoughts are still on the negative side.

> But I, O LORD, cry to thee;
> in the morning my prayer comes before thee.
> O LORD, why dost thou cast me off?
> Why dost thou hide thy face from me?
> Afflicted and close to death from my youth up,
> I suffer thy terrors; I am helpless.
> Thy wrath has swept over me;
> thy dread assaults destroy me.

They surround me like a flood all day long;
    they close in upon me together.
Thou hast caused lover and friend to shun me;
    my companions are in darkness.
    (Psalm 88:13-18, RSV)

The psalmist is sharing his negative feelings about God with God. He is not alone. This is a cathartic and healing experience. This psalmist, like Nouwen, is able to describe his pain to God because of his intuitive conviction or awareness that God understands. In his depression, he is having a lover's quarrel with God. He is actively engaged in the relationship, which is a healthy antidepressant for him.

Prayer keeps one's depression dialogical in one's solitude. Such prayer not only prevents the depression from deepening, but is also a way of lifting the depression. Pastoral counseling has as its resources the Scriptures and prayer, which can be used with great benefit together.

Philosopher Mortimer Adler was in the hospital for many months with a viral infection. During this time he experienced depression, often crying uncontrollably as depressed persons often do. An Episcopal priest called on him and prayed for him. Adler choked up and wept some more. After this prayer, Adler began praying the only prayer he knew, the Lord's Prayer. He prayed it repeatedly. Then he realized that he was praying for the first time in his life. "Quite suddenly when I awoke one night, a light dawned on me, and I realized what had happened without my recognizing it clearly then. . . . I had been praying to God."

He rang for the night nurse and asked for paper and pen. He scribbled a note, asking the priest to call on him at home when he left the hospital. He did and Adler was baptized at his home in the presence of his wife. He became a convert to Christianity at age eighty-two. It all began with a pastoral prayer (Mortimer Adler, *A Second Look through the Rear View Mirror*, New York: Macmillan, 1992, pages. 276-77).

*Electroconvulsive Therapy (ECT)*

Another valuable treatment for the seriously depressed is electroconvulsive therapy (ECT), or shock treatments. These are given when needed to the clinically depressed. In their present sophisticated form, the treatments are not at all uncomfortable to receive. The patient is given a muscle relaxant and is sedated for the experience. A small amount of electric current is then run through the brain for a very short time. It is always administered by trained psychiatrists.

Based on my experience, there is no reason to fear shock treatments or to have any sense of shame for having taken them. Those who tell about negative experiences with shock treatments usually base their opinions on what happened some time ago. There has been much improvement in shock treatments since then. ECT has had a resurgence in recent years because of the improvements and also because it works effectively for the great majority of people.

Now a much smaller amount of electricity is used in shock treatments than heretofore. Muscle relaxants prevent any harm to the body from the convulsion, and the sedative prevents any unpleasant memory. The amount of time for a shock treatment has also been reduced, with the whole procedure taking just a few minutes. ECT was a godsend for me and may well have saved my life. Some people have experienced memory loss due to these treatments, but usually because they received more than the normal six to nine treatments. In my case, I experienced no memory loss and can even remember everything about the treatments except for the brief time when I was unconscious from the sedation.

ECT is only given at some mental hospitals and some mental units of general hospitals. It also can be administered on an outpatient basis, should a person need follow-up after hospitalization. A hospital's purpose is to give the patient what he or she cannot get otherwise. For the depressed person, this means surveillance, ECT, and a variety of therapeutic activities conducted on a corporate basis within the mental unit (when my depression was at its worst, I chose not to participate in any of them). Hospitals have their limits, however, as has already been stated.

Shock treatments are followed by medication for six months as a preventative treatment. During this time, people are encouraged to engage in healthy mental, physical, spiritual, and social activities.

## Pet Therapy

For people living alone, especially the elderly, having a pet can be a antidepressant. Cats, dogs, and birds can take on human proportions for those who care for them. A pet can provide the company that all of us need. Boris Levinson, the father of pet therapy, says, "A pet is an island of sanity in what appears to be an insane world." Because older people can put their trust and friendship into their pets, a person may look upon his or her pet as "a significant other." In addition, taking care of pets instills feelings of accomplishment and self-respect (Maureen Drummond-Scannell and Tammy Feo-Garchar, "Pets," *Healthy Connections*, Winter 1994, pages 2-3).

# FIVE

## *Managing Depression*

 A HEALTHY LIFESTYLE IS an effective antidepressant because it involves the spiritual, mental, physical, and social aspects of life. It is helpful both in preventing depressions and in healing them.

A study was done of centenarians living on their own, some of them still working (*20/20*, ABC television, July 18, 1993). After extensive observations and interviewing, the researchers concluded that these people all had several things in common. Those included a positive attitude, the ability to adapt to loss, and involvement in life. As one would suspect, these older people did not have the chronic depression that some other older people have.

Preventatives related to lifestyle are helpful but they do not always completely prevent depression. In my case, I practiced all of those things I will describe in this chapter prior to my clinical depression, but they did not prevent it from happening. Nonetheless, I have continued to practice them and to encourage my students and counselees to do so, at the same time reminding them that there are no guarantees.

### SPIRITUAL HEALTH

Our mental, physical, and spiritual health are all interrelated in the biblical sense of who we are as human beings. The wholism of the Bible long preceded our current resurrection of the idea. In depression, one's spirit is affected as well as one's mind and body.

Devoting some time each day to our spiritual health, especially to prayer and Bible meditation, is an antidepressant. Doing so helps to cultivate a daily habit of prayer time, which helps keep one's spirits up. Prayer and meditation are also antidotes to stress, which is often related to depression. As an old prayer puts it, "Give us thoughts that pass into prayers." This was a key for the psalmists' overcoming of their depressions. Their thoughts were constantly put into dialogue with God.

When Jesus was in agony in the Garden of Gethsemane, knowing the crucifixion awaited him the next day, he prayed to his heavenly Father. He brought all his thoughts and feelings to God through prayers of petition. He even asked that he be spared the cross. However, knowing why he was sent to earth, he also prayed that God's will be done. He arose from those prayers strengthened to go to the cross.

When we are emotionally disturbed, it may help us to pray out loud in order to drain our emotions. We don't have to be concerned about praying in a nice way. After all, God knows our thoughts and feelings and expressing them to God is therapeutic for us. Even when our anger is against God (or the way things are going in our life), we can express it fully in prayer. God can not only take it, but also understands.

Because I am a committed Christian, I sought therapies for depression that include a spiritual focus. I was asked by a veteran at a veterans' home if I could explain how to cope with depression and leave God out. I said I could not. I was a guest of the chaplain's department so there was no problem with my answer. While the doctors who were present were not witnessing Christians, they were respectful of my opinion. I have not arrived at my Christian position without a struggle. If my experience is not unusual, I would guess that most clergy struggle with their faith. As one pastor father told his daughter, "You will be a good pastor because faith has not come easily to you."

Because we tend to focus only on our own pains, which give us a distorted picture of life, it is important always to include prayers of intercession for others. Depression, like all pain, tends to turn us in on ourselves. We need to take time to think of our fellow sufferers among our acquaintances and pray for them. It may be helpful to keep a written list of these people. In this way, we are not only helping them, but we are broadening our vision, which is a healthy thing to do. It breaks our focus on ourselves, at least for the moment, as we focus on the needs of others.

We are to pray for ourselves, too, of course, making specific petitions. If we are feeling down or even depressed, we can pray, "God, lift my mood. God, take away my depression."

Sometimes in our depressive thinking, we do not pray for our recovery simply because we do not see any hope. There are times when praying for healing seems useless to the depressed mind. But we still could pray for healing, and our pastors could encourage this.

When we are depressed, we tend to focus on what we do not have rather than what we do have. During our down times, our perspective is distorted and we focus on our debits and overlook our blessings. This is a frequent characteristic of depressive thinking. Often the attitude or quality of gratitude is gone.

That's why prayer time needs to include praise time. This is the time when we thank God specifically for all the blessings we normally take for granted. This keeps our perspective balanced. Praise time generates a creative tension between our blessings and our needs. It helps to keep us rational. A devotional time is still helpful as an antidepressant during our down times, and our negative thoughts are usually lessened by such persistence. When we are persistent, our desire to pray will return.

When we do pray, we should follow the structure outlined by Paul in Philippians 4:6: "Do not worry [be depressed] about anything, but in everything by prayer and supplication *with thanksgiving* let your requests be made known to God." In other words, forcing ourselves to give thanks makes our depressed mind expand its vision. This gives us a more realistic view of our lives, seeing what we have as well as what we do not have.

I have followed this procedure in my pastoral counseling with depressed people. As I read the above passage to one counselee, she heard the words "with thanksgiving," and said, "I don't have anything to be thankful for."

I took a sheet of paper and said, "I am going to list all the assets that you have that you would not want to give up. First your eyes. You can see. You wouldn't want to be blind, would you?"

"No," she replied.

"Your ears," I continued, "you would not want to be deaf, would you?"

"No," she said.

"You didn't come in here in a wheelchair; you walked in. You wouldn't want to be confined to a wheelchair, would you?"

Again, she replied, "No."

So I continued until I had quite a list. Then I said, "I'm going to give you this list and every day when you pray for your depression to lift, I want you to go over this list and thank God for every blessing on here."

When she returned for the next counseling session, she said, "You know, after I finish that list, I feel better."

"That's what St. Paul said would happen," I said, and quoted the following verse: "And the peace of God, which passes all understanding, will guard your hearts and your minds in Christ Jesus" (Philippians 4:7).

Gratitude is perhaps the most spiritual of our attitudes because it turns us to the Source of our blessings. We are grateful to someone. When we are grateful for our life and all its blessings, we have within our spirit a strong antidepressant. Praising God, which is an expression of gratitude, is good for our spirits.

Prayer is speaking to God; meditation is the listening phase of prayer. As preparation for this listening, make a conscious effort to relax your body, beginning with your toes and working up the legs and back to shoulders and arms and fingers. Visualize the muscles in each of these letting go and becoming relaxed. Then in this relaxed state, entertain silence. In this silence, you may want to focus on something like a picture of Jesus or on the words of Jesus. Use your cognitive behavior skills (see page 85 in this chapter) to keep out distractions and to return to your silent focus.

Because meditation is the listening phase of prayer and God speaks to us through the Bible, focus on a Bible verse; one that means much to you, perhaps one that you have memorized. Stay with it, listening for a brief moment and then go to another verse. Well-known scriptures like Psalm 23 and the Lord's Prayer can also be used, pausing after each verse or petition and listening in silence.

You can send prayers of petition to God during meditation by sending mind pictures. For example, if you are interceding for a friend in pain, then see that friend healed and inwardly say "Amen" to that picture. You can do the same for yourself. See the picture of yourself healed and again silently say "Amen."

## SOCIAL INTERACTION

Social interaction with people is another antidepressant. That is why depressed people should avoid being alone and why cognitive behavioral therapy stresses socializing. As we keep our balance in living by cultivating our friendships and socializing regularly, we are doing something to forestall depression. If one is married, other couples can be included so that one's spouse participates in one's friendships and socializing. There are many things friends can do together—going to sporting events, concerts, movies, and plays, as well as eating out together. But the important thing is allowing time after the events to discuss them together.

The congregation of believers can be a great help both for socializing and for spiritual growth. Being with persons who hold and practice the same values sharpens our will and ability to apply common values. As with our family of origin, the church offers both blessing and irritation. Becoming open and vulnerable in a wider area gives us a learning experience; we find that community rather than dominance is not easy to achieve. In this setting we face the usual threats to community and learn to apply our interpersonal skills as Christians.

In small-group meetings where there is a planned goal of spiritual growth, true feelings and experiences are put into words. The value of verbalizing feelings is that understanding follows. Our fellow believers understand us and we understand ourselves better. In any group where intimate experiences are verbalized with open hearts, we create fellowship and deepen our understanding of bearing each other's burdens.

## Physical Health

Regular physical exercise is also an antidepressant. Research has found that runners, for example, have less depression than non-runners. When the body reaches a certain buildup in physical exertion, it releases endorphins into the physical system, which are nature's own mood-lifters or antidepressants. Of course, we cannot all be runners. Swimming is excellent, as are bicycling (including using stationary bicycles) and brisk walking. The main thing is that we do what we can do and do it regularly. As has been said regarding the physical limitations of some people, "If you can move it, move it!"

Food and good nutrition are also important in keeping our physical self fit and healthy. Our physiological cell structure is dependent on what we ingest into our body for its proper functioning. In our land of plenty, we have malnutrition not only because of poverty, but also because of poor eating choices. While overweight, we can be starved for the food that our cells need, and that includes our brain cells. Focusing on vegetables and fruit will keep the center of our diet healthy. What good nutrition has to do with preventing depression has not been clearly established, but it does have a lot to do with keeping our bodies healthy. That by itself is a depression preventative.

It is important to trace all negative feelings, including feelings of stress, to their origin in your thoughts. Then examine those thoughts as to their accuracy, rationality, and helpfulness. If they are inaccurate, irrational, or unhelpful, which they usually are, evict them. You do have the power to do this. Then replace the faulty thought with an accurate, rational, and helpful thought. You also have the power do this.

For example, if your negative feelings are being fed by the thought that you aren't appreciated at your workplace, make yourself deal only with the facts and not impressions you may have been projecting onto those thoughts. Then replace the faulty thought with "Perhaps I am more appreciated than I realize, and I am going to go on that principle until it is proved otherwise." You will need to do this repeatedly and relentlessly, even though there are no immediate results in your feelings. But with persistence you will see positive benefits.

Feelings follow thoughts eventually, though there is a time lag that can be discouraging. Again, you have the power to trace the thought that leads to discouraged feelings. In other words, you do not need to tolerate discouragement. By using this discipline with your thoughts, you will clean up your mental "insides." If you sense God calling you in this direction, you will find it easier to act on this discipline.

Along this same line, cleaning out "the museum of past hurts" is a helpful step. If you are carrying within you resentments from the past, they are like poison to your mental health. So, for your own sake, forgive those who have hurt you so that you can come to peace with the past. As Søren Kierkegaard said, it is not the forgiven who is blest, but the forgiver. So forgive for your sake.

Clear out all your relational systems. By this I mean if there is unfinished business in any of your significant relationships, work for reconciliation. Do all you can to unblock the channels that connect you so that your love can flow again through them. If your efforts fail, it is no longer your problem. Let the other person bear his or her own responsibility. After you have made all efforts toward reconciliation and have failed, it is irrational to feel guilty about the relationship. You need to evict such guilty thoughts.

By the same token, clean out your own system in your relationship with yourself. All unresolved guilt and shame should be faced and dealt with in terms of God's unconditional forgiveness. See yourself in your imagination offering this guilt and shame to Jesus, and see Jesus throw them far out of sight. Do this over and over again until they are gone. Now that they are gone, let them go. God wants you to be free from all unresolved guilt and shame so that you will feel good about yourself. That will contribute much to your mental health.

You will encounter new problems. As life moves on, it brings them. But they don't need to be mixed up and confused with old problems. These old problems need resolution and reconciliation so that you can leave them where they belong—in a nonthreatening past. St. Paul saw clearly that reconciliation with God enables us to do precisely this—leave the old and enter the new. "So if anyone is in Christ, there is a new creation: everything old has passed away; see, everything has become new! All this is from God, who reconciled us to himself through Christ" (2 Corinthians 5:17-18).

*Involvement in Work and Creative Activities*

All of us need to get out of ourselves and beyond ourselves for our mental health, and a major way to do this is to become involved in creative activities. For some people, their work supplies sufficient challenge for their creative needs. Others need to find projects that they do in addition to their work. If our work is not satisfying these needs, we either need to look for another job or find suitable outlets through our church or community. If we look around, we can find places where our efforts can help in some way that we believe is important and worthwhile. When this need to give of ourselves, this need to be creative, is blocked, we are inviting depression.

*Cognitive Behavioral Therapy*

The value I received in learning to use cognitive behavioral therapy (CBT) actually made my situational depression over my Ménière's disease worthwhile. I continue to use CBT not only as a counteractive to depressive thoughts, but also to counteract stress, bad feelings toward others, anger, and any general mental loss of moorings. I find in cognitive therapy a source of power, of self-control or self-discipline under God. The words of 2 Timothy 1:7 (RSV) express what I have discovered: "For God did not give us a spirit of timidity but a spirit of power and love and self-control." In other words, God has given us power to love by giving us the power of self-control. I have found this power implemented by my use of cognitive therapy.

To maintain this self-control under God, it is important to keep our feelings in the forefront of our consciousness. Once we have identified our feelings, we can trace their origin to the thoughts in our mind. When we have located the thought, we give it the threefold test: Is it rational, is it accurate, and is it helpful? If it fails to pass this test, we use our power of self-control to evict it from our mind and to replace it with a rational, accurate, and helpful thought. In this way we are working to clean up our mind and will be rewarded shortly by the good feelings that go with the better thoughts.

As I continue to use CBT when I need it, which is almost daily and nightly, the time lag between the change of thoughts and the resurgence of good feelings is getting shorter. Sometimes the lag ends in the same day.

Cognitive therapy is a way of reframing things in healthy ways; this keeps my mind positive. St. Paul was one of the original positive thinkers. In Philippians 4:8, he wrote, "Finally, beloved, whatever is true, whatever is honorable, whatever is just, whatever is pure, whatever is pleasing, whatever is commendable, if there is any excellence and if there is anything worthy of praise, think about these things."

Our growth into a healthy lifestyle could also be described as a process of working out the domination of what we call "the law," and what cultural analyst Karen Horney calls "the tyranny of the should," into the gospel of God's unconditional love as the *modus operandi* for daily living. The gospel of God's forgiving love is an antidepressant, while the law without the gospel can lead to depression through its creation of guilt and shame.

When we live by the gospel, the pressure is off; we don't have to prove anything. We begin with the gift of our worth and live in the warmth and security of God's unconditional and incarnated love as revealed in Jesus. It is a process because we are continually growing out of something (law) into something (gospel). The law of judgment has such a hold on us because, as the theologians say, we are sinners, and the law is "nature's" way of coping with our sinfulness. But the main accomplishment of the law is that it creates guilt, which it leaves unresolved, and shame, which blights our entire outlook on life. The gospel is an alternative way of coping with our sinfulness because God removes all guilt and shame through divine forgiveness, giving us freedom for creating new life in the future.

The law leaves us feeling alone, condemned, and hopeless—all likely ingredients for the creation of depression. To help us realize the gospel at these times, I suggest that you visualize God's arms coming from the cross of Christ and embracing you as you are. Even though at the moment such an action may seem foreign to your feelings, do it regardless, forcing yourself if necessary. The process is lifelong, but genuine progress can be made so that whatever loneliness, judgment, and hopelessness you have are continually challenged by love, joy, and peace.

## LEARNING MORE ABOUT DEPRESSION

Our current cultural values and priorities contribute to the onset of depression. Our culture, which we could identify as stressing the "law," implies that we always need to prove our worth. The Christian gospel and what it teaches stand as the exact opposite of our culture and its values. In this section we shall look at the damage our culture inflicts by emphasizing competition, extroversion, and intelligence, and how our culture's values affect women.

## Our Culture's Emphasis on Competition

We live in a hostile environment of competition. We are under pressure to compete to stay afloat, and when we do, we often find ourselves hopeless in the competition. The stress that results from this is the front door to depression. As I write this, Lucy and I have just been watching the winter Olympics on television. We marveled at those athletes' control of their minds and bodies, particularly those who won medals, especially the gold. But the athletic stars of the world are at the top of a huge pyramid of others who didn't make it, either in skating or in other ventures of life. They are not featured on television but rather are hidden in the sorrows of failure.

When we compete, our competitors are the enemy. Their bad luck is our good fortune. It takes more maturity than most of us have to do our best and still respect others. Loving our neighbor is more difficult when that neighbor is in competition with us.

Competition leads to comparisons. Ours is an upwardly mobile society. Each of us is confronted with pressure to climb the ladder of success. We experience anguish as we think that we may fail to get very high or that we may even fall off the ladder. Our highly competitive society cuts into the experience of human community. If I am in competition with you, I will not let you see my vulnerability lest you take advantage of me; therefore I cannot let myself get close to you. People under pressure to compete are always comparing themselves with others in the competitive milieu. And when they are suffering from a sense of failure, they see others as more competent, self-possessed, and happy than they themselves are. Of course, they are looking through the distorted lens of their own put-down.

When we make such comparisons, we are taking over the role of judge over what is good and right about ourselves. In that experience we often leave behind thankfulness for what we have. Thankfulness is sometimes mistaken for conceit. If we are pleased with what God has given us, the assumption is that we will not strive to improve. But contrary to the put-down comparison, we have moved into a springboard of strength by appreciating, with humility, our God-given gifts.

We don't escape the tendency to make comparisons in the theological seminary where I have taught. Recently a student sought my counsel for a mild depression. Soon we discovered that the main problem was the highly competitive climate at the seminary. Because the student lacked some of the sophisticated background of some of his classmates, he felt inferior to them.

"I'm always comparing," he said, "and always coming out on the short end. In class I don't dare say anything for fear it will sound stupid."

"How do you see these others?" I asked.

"Very self-assured and confident, the exact opposite of me."

"How do you know?" I asked.

He paused and then said, "I guess I just assume it."

"Right," I said, "but because you are seeing distortedly; you are making some wrong assumptions. They are fellow human beings who feel the same fears as you do. Only they don't show it; or at least not enough so that you can pick it up."

I continued, "Do you know what St. Paul said about those who compare themselves with others?"

"No," he said.

So I read to him 2 Corinthians 10:12b, "But when they measure themselves by one another, and compare themselves with one another, they do not show good sense."

"How can I stop?" he asked.

"You have already taken the first step by seeing the need to stop. From now on, it is a matter of throwing these comparing thoughts out of your mind whenever they invade it. Hear God calling you to do this."

As with this student, competitiveness can lead to negative self-judgment, low self-esteem, and ultimately to depression. The cultural values and priorities that fortify this emphasis on making comparisons are internalized by us so that they become our own. Through our distorted vision, others also appear to be much more self-possessed than we are. This down-on-me attitude is an early symptom of depression.

One of the popular antidotes to depression has been to look for someone who has less than we do or someone whose problems are worse than ours are. The problem with this tactic is that it distorts both our situation and that of the other person. Comparisons can be made only of observable behavior, and that means that we have to be objective about ourselves and others. Only God knows all the situations objectively. Therefore, to "rejoice with those who rejoice, and weep with those who weep" is the appropriate response. When reality is discovered, empathy, not self-satisfaction, is a more likely response.

Our society teaches us to be open to receiving communication as long as that communication is nonthreatening. However, because we are always in competition with one another, the communication is usually threatening. This leads us to forms of protection such as facades and interpersonal isolation, both of which promote depression.

Eric Berne, who developed transactional analysis, said that our greetings as we meet one another are pastimes, not to be taken seriously. I believe they are more than pastimes. Rather they are symbols of the pressures on us to adopt only positive messages. They are also forms of protection. To test this hypothesis, the next time someone says, "How are you?" answer, "Lousy!" This throws the other off balance. He or she does not know how to respond. You failed to play the game.

Each cover-up or facade makes us more unreal to ourselves. Eventually we are out of touch with some areas of ourselves. Our religion asks us to be in touch with our true self, the self that is comfortable with God and the one we know is out of touch. Being out of touch may begin in childhood. By expecting our children to conform to our ambitious picture of them, we are asking them to cover up and build a facade to please us, rather than helping them find their true center. Our judgment of them has discouraged them.

As we have seen, competition because of the pressure to conceal weaknesses may lead to interpersonal isolation, a breeding ground for depression. In one's isolation, one feels the pangs of loneliness, fear, and anxiety. Only when one can cease comparing and begin relating to others as they are will the cultural tendency to depression lift.

## Our Culture's Bias toward Extroversion

The well-known Myers-Briggs Type Indicator reflects values that contrast with those of our culture. The four categories of the inventory are thinking-feeling, perception-judgment, extroversion-introversion, and sensing-intuition. It recognizes that all types of persons, and all combinations of those categories, including extroversion and introversion, have equal value.

Our culture strongly values extroversion. In a former day, an excessively extroverted person might have been considered shallow. Today with the high value we place on salesmanship and the ability to do well in front of people, we seldom ask that a person be reflective or a deep thinker. In fact, one writer declared that the drug Prozac seems "to lend the introvert the social skills of a salesman," implying that introverts need to change (Norman Brown, "Defeating Depression," *Northwest Airlines World Traveler*, March 1994, page 72).

The experiences of people with strong tendencies toward introversion or toward extroversion are not the same. Introverts often feel judged and isolated because, if nothing else, their number is smaller. Introverts' awareness of the nature of their environment can lead them to make some necessary adjustments. Many find that joining groups and learning acceptable social skills helps them be able to reach out to others. When people are accepted by their peers, depression and loneliness lift. One reason that introverts are more inclined to depression than extroverts may be that they miss out on some self-understanding that contacts with a wide range of people could give them. Social settings are less appealing to them.

Introverts learn very early that they do not see things the way the majority of people do. Even in the family, parents who are quite extroverted do not always understand their more reflective and less outgoing children. After all, our culture tells us that being outgoing and extroverted is much more acceptable.

The Myers-Briggs Type Indicator can be very helpful to families that take it. Parents can better understand any of their children who differ from them and accept them as they are. Keenly observant leaders have always been aware of how to maximize the contributions of those they lead. It is time today to give our societal support to both extroverts and introverts.

## Our Culture's Emphasis on Intelligence

Ours also is a culture that favors those who are bright intellectually. What does this do to children who do not do well in school? One-fourth of our children have some kind of learning disability, dyslexia being the most common. Such disabilities can be extremely frustrating to the children who have them because parents and teachers often do not recognize the disabilities for what they are.

An eighteen-year-old young woman came to see me for counseling for a mild depression. Because she lacked insight into herself and her situation, it took quite a while to get to the heart of her problem. She was finally able to tell me about a trauma she experienced in the ninth grade. Classes were such a miserable experience for her that she often skipped them and went to the library instead. Convinced she was stupid, she found little sympathy from her teachers or her parents. Both were frustrated with her and kept urging her to try harder. But because she had a severe case of dyslexia (although no one knew that at the time), trying harder didn't work. Being a child of a religious home, she prayed for help, but no help came. This caused a spiritual crisis as well, for God too had failed her. In utter frustration, she quit school, much to everyone's disgust.

Through testing, her learning disability was identified as dyslexia. Now she is getting help from the public school system and is working toward her GED. Hope has returned to her again, and her self-image has risen considerably. "I now know what was wrong," she said. "And I know I am not stupid and that I can get help for my problem."

## OUR CULTURE'S EFFECT ON WOMEN

Women seem to be more depression prone than men, and some of our culture's values and emphases may be contributing factors.

Women are especially vulnerable when comparisons are made. For instance, the norm for a beautiful female body is culturally set by the media. Most women cannot measure up to that norm. Women constantly see sophisticated photography of female bodies made to appeal to men, whose tastes are also culturally set. Sexual aspects are emphasized, with the breasts, hips, legs, hair, mouth, and lips designed for sexual gratification. The models seem to be getting younger and younger.

Women with impressionable minds (and we all have them) decide subconsciously that their bodies are inferior, or in rare instances, equal or superior to the images the media presents. The illusion of inferiority or superiority is reinforced by our culture, which recognizes impressions above substance. A minor depression can deepen if a woman makes an unfavorable comparison of her body with the media's ideal. Young women are most strongly affected. Something is "wrong" with them and must be corrected or accepted as inferior. The first judgment or evaluation of a woman in our culture seems to be how she looks, particularly her attractiveness to males as prescribed by the media.

Women are prone to comparisons in the early years of marriage and child rearing. This period of growth is often marked by lack of self-confidence. As women are thrust together in groups of their peers, the obvious measuring that goes on can precipitate depression. Such comparisons and judgments often continue through all the stages of life. For older women, discussions can center around comparisons of their adult children. Friendships can end when conversations degenerate into comparing children and grandchildren. The challenge is to accept our own situation as it is, and to accept our own (if we have some) or others' children or grandchildren as having true and inherent worth as children of God who are growing in grace.

Our culture has many values that cause women problems. The pride a girl or woman may have in her intellect may take a trouncing. In educational settings, all are compared favorably or unfavorably to a standard of high grades, yet in some cases, women are labeled less feminine if they do well. In the work world, a woman's worth is often determined by her ability to find a suitable job.

Without a strong home background to support them or role models to guide them, and with our culture's values and priorities beckoning them, many young women may see little reason to postpone sexual gratification. But early parenthood and even marriage can be dead-end streets. Many of the programs designed to deal with early parenting are also designed to lift depression. Feeling trapped and believing the future is bleak can create anger, and those feelings can lead to depression. Single mothers may feel especially burdened because it may seem to them that schools and other institutions are prejudiced against their children.

With some women, it is hard to tell what the root of their depression is. Depression may result from our culture's values, including its emphasis on comparisons, but depression may also be associated with a woman's physiology. This, of course, varies considerably from woman to woman. Even when unencumbered by physiological changes, a woman can still become depressed when "things go wrong."

In many women, the menstrual cycle is accompanied by depression. It is aggravated by the fact that some women have difficulty controlling their behavior during these times, and being out of control is unnerving. One woman commented, "There are several days each month that I do not like myself."

Premenstrual syndrome (PMS), a difficult experience for many women, can include depression. Despite the difficulty of living through the difficult times associated with hormonal changes, women continue to feel responsibility for their husbands, children, and their own personal success. This aggravates the depressive aspects of PMS.

Women can also suffer depression in connection with childbirth. Postpartum depression is not uncommon, and prepartum depression, while more rare, does occur. It can take years for such depressive experiences to be processed. The experience of childbirth reduces women to positions of dependency and it may seem to them that they have to start over in gaining self-confidence. As someone said, "Childbirth and infant care are very humbling experiences."

Today's women often feel they have to be as competitive as their male counterparts in the workplace. Yet studies show that in households where women are employed outside the home, most of the housework and management of the home still falls to them.

Women, when they feel depressed or worried, do tend to seek out friends and professional help sooner than men. But with both work and home to manage and balance, women have less time to share with other women than they did in the past.

## Our Culture's Values or the Gospel's?

So many of our culture's values can harm us, and many of them seem to pave the way to depression as our worth is questioned again and again. What we need to remember is the gospel. The good news that comes through Christ assures us that our worth is a gift to us from our beginning.

The Sacrament of Baptism in those churches that baptize infants is the focal point of this reception of worth. Through the sacrament, we are assured of God's unconditional love for us—a love that will never leave us in our most unlovable moments. This leaves us with nothing to prove, nothing to work out.

This is the releasing message that people in our society need desperately to hear and believe. Once we identify with the values of the gospel, we can see that the values of our culture are big lies. But since we Christians live in this world, we are influenced by it so that we too experience the pressures of our culture's demands. This is why we need constantly to refresh our minds by recalling the freedom of our heritage so that we can resist the pressures of our culture on us.

Therefore the preaching of the gospel, as well as its communication in teaching and pastoral care and counseling, are effective depression preventatives in counteracting the influence of our culture on us. Jesus said that we are to be in the world but not of it. That is a difficult tension within which to live. Yet it is the one way to avoid the depression caused by the cultural pressure we face to prove ourselves. Christianity is by its very nature counter-cultural, and it is also an antidepressant. Regular church attendance immerses us in this gospel and therefore it is probably one of the best habits that we can develop to prevent depression.

# Six

## How You Can Help

FAMILIES, FRIENDS, AND CLERGY are affected when people become depressed. In this chapter, we will direct our remarks to them because there are ways they can help depressed persons in their recovery. For the first two sections, Bill will speak first to the identified groups; and Lucy will give her insights as related to our situation.

### Bill speaks

*The Family*

The family of the depressed person may be the key to his or her recovery. The family needs to take hold when the depressed family member does not think help is possible. Overwhelmed by hopelessness, the person may make poor decisions regarding any treatment. So the family may need to make those decisions for the depressed person.

Family members need not be frightened should their loved one need hospitalization. That is what hospitals are for, to give treatment that cannot be given at home and to provide surveillance. Find out before admittance what kind of surveillance there will be and what other precautions against suicide are taken. Your family doctor or psychiatrist can help you determine which hospital would be the best and can also help with admittance. Then get your loved one out of the hospital as soon as he or she begins to show sufficient improvement to return home. Hospitals do not generally provide a very healing ambiance.

As you recall in our case, because I had improved so much, the hospital offered a home overnight visit. Lucy was not at ease with this so she negotiated a shorter visit. Getting adjusted to being at home was a crucial step in my healing, so a welcoming attitude was necessary even though Lucy had fears about being able to handle it. Both the patient and the family will feel anxiety. We were only a short distance from the hospital so our anxiety was minimal. A family and patient who lived further away would have to make careful decisions.

While your loved one is in the hospital, visit him or her every day if possible, even if there is no response to your visits. Cooperate with the staff in the treatment that is provided, even shock treatments if the psychiatrist recommends them. Particularly in the unit for the severely disturbed, I noticed that hardly any of those patients ever received visitors. As I look back, I realize now that the family visits were good for me even though I discouraged them.

Be alert to the care that is given. Ask about it and check on it. In a watchdog way, you need to be your loved one's own "doctor." Family members are a patient's advocates. Ask questions about medications, for example, and about their side effects. Don't assume the proper care is being given. Do your own research at the hospital and on the subject of depression. Recall how Lucy did all these things as she described in chapter one. They all proved to be very necessary.

In these ways you become a real partner with the hospital staff. Don't fight them—that doesn't work. Make the effort in a respectful way to find out what is going on and to get the necessary action. Check your loved one's food intake to see if he or she is eating sufficiently and drinking adequately. Also get information about the person's bowel movements, for these can also become a problem in healing.

As you recall from chapter two, when Lucy became alarmed about my not drinking or eating, she persevered in her efforts to have intravenous liquids and a feeding tube added to my treatment. This is a major decision for a doctor, since in my case it meant my transference to the unit for the severely disturbed, and that is not a nice place to be. I'm sure he appreciated Lucy's support to take that action. I found out later that he talked to my pastoral counselor, Bill Smith, to see if he could persuade me to cooperate more, especially by eating and drinking.

It was our experience that all of the staff appreciated having the support of a concerned family. This was true particularly in the mental unit where so many patients are neglected by their families, probably because of what they believe is the stigma of mental illness (see pages 107-110 in this chapter).

## Lucy speaks

### The Family

In my experience of Bill's illness, I had not only my own concerns but those of our adult children as well as Bill's only sibling, his brother. Fortunately our relationship with him was good. I called Bill's brother, who lived quite a distance away, and told him everything because I wanted him to feel a part of the immediate family and not left out. He was straight with me and did not question any of my decisions. It would have been trying for me if he had chosen to be difficult; that would have made it harder for him to trust my actions.

At an earlier age, I would have been very vulnerable to family pressures. I also would have been much more sensitive to the societal stigma that surrounds mental illness and would have become more entangled with my own emotions. I believe I handled the situation with our family maturely. This enabled all of us to put whatever knowledge we had together.

It was important for my future and my family's future not to hear later, "If I had known more, Bill could have had better care," or some similar conclusion. Bill's brother did not question my assessment that Bill was in the best possible facility and that his physicians could not have been better. That was important to me.

So with each family member, I made sure that I repeated accurately all that I knew. We had a daughter and a son who were living far from us and kept them informed. I knew from my own siblings how entangling relationships can become at times like these, and how they can sometimes become impossible to straighten out. I knew that the best course of action for all of us was to give complete and accurate information. Family members need to know of the situation as completely as possible because they have to readjust to the person when the healing comes.

Speaking over the phone long distance has its limitations. Since I am accustomed to being very brief, sometimes misinterpretations occurred. We all had to accept that this was a time of serious trouble unlike any we had faced before, and that it was important for all of us to be in accord. We had a loved one in the hospital, and the predicted outcome was not totally positive. The fact that ten percent of depression sufferers are not cured by shock treatments had to be faced by us, even though we did not share this with outsiders. Nothing that we could see caused us to doubt the doctor's hope that Bill would be in the ninety percent, which was more of a certainty than I had had with other medical problems. It was wonderful to be able to trust that if anything could be done, it was being done.

The time came when Bill would not cooperate at all and no alternatives were left except shock treatments. It was at that time that there was a division in the family. Our oldest son, Dale, felt strongly that his dad, after wrestling with so many problems—his illness, his approaching retirement, and the spiritual crisis caused by these—would begin to come out of his depression. Our youngest daughter had worked in mental hospitals where shock treatments sometimes had not worked; she even believed that sometimes they were used punitively. She felt that other methods should be used and more time taken. None of us really knew much about ECT. Library articles that I had read were very positive about them. Some of the children wanted to see if medication might still work, even though the psychiatrists told us that Bill could not wait the six weeks needed for improvement. Naturally, we wished that ECT could have been avoided. Of course another bit of denial (and a major problem) was that Bill refused to take any medication.

Our children were surprisingly objective with their father. They and their spouses were neither ashamed of him nor intimidated by his illness, nor did they ever doubt that their father would recover. They finally accepted the doctor's word, as had I, and cooperated in every way they could.

Our in-town children were very good about visiting Bill. Being there helped keep denial at a minimum. Family members need to know how far a patient has to go to be healed, and they must believe that healing will happen. I believe that our frequent consultations kept us closer to him; he was never out of our daily concern.

Our frequent visits also made us more appreciative of the staff. Seeing the conditions and frustrations of working with the mentally ill is very instructive. A number of the patients had to be reminded of the boundaries between them and others. Many of them, in contrast to Bill, verbalized their delusions constantly and kept up perpetual motion, often walking and talking nonstop. The cultural backgrounds varied from professional to laborer to unemployed. None of them were themselves, and they required the staff to be very versatile.

In contrast to the hospital staff, family members really know the patient. When a nurse asked me, "Was your husband often despairing?" I assured her that this was most unusual for him. Bill received many cards from friends and I kept them in a box on his bed table. I would read them to him and left them, hoping he would take the initiative to read them himself, which of course he never did. When a nurse asked me what was in the box, I said that it contained cards from friends. She replied, looking surprised, "I didn't think that he would have any friends."

A particularly cherished event during this troubled time was when our son and daughter-in-law invited the rest of the family to a party for a friend who had just returned from Antarctica. It was a wonderful break from the stress. In his paranoia, Bill could not believe there was such a party when we told him about it. He "knew" that our son and his wife were now divorced, and he could not believe they would come together for such an occasion.

## Bill speaks

*Friends*

As a friend of a person who is hospitalized for depression, call on him or her unless the family discourages it. My friends could not call on me because I had a strict "no visitors" rule and my family concurred. This, of course, was my right in the hospital. Whether it was wise or not, I really don't know. I do know that it was a favor to my friends who may not have known how to handle my rejection. Yet the fact remains that depressed people need people whether they know it or not.

When you visit, keep the visit short. Listen to your friend if he or she is willing to talk. Otherwise sit with him or her in a relaxed presence. Just being there is important. When you leave, give your friend a reasonable hope. "I believe you are going to get better. Lean on my faith. You are going to make it. God bless you."

When your friend is in the hospital, respect the limitation if there are to be no visitors. You, of course, will want to know how your friend is doing. One way to do this is to call the family at home. But if all the person's friends did this, the poor spouse and others would be driven to distraction answering the phone. After the spouse or family members come home from the hospital, being bombarded with phone calls only adds to the stress. I recall our son Lance, who stayed with Lucy for two weeks when he came from Germany, telling me that our phone was ringing off the hook, and he said it in a very distraught manner.

Since at least some of the friends of a depressed person know each other, they can organize a phone-calling schedule with one appointed to call each day or two and to report to the others. This would spare the spouse and others in the home much additional stress. However, the person must be one who can be trusted for accurate reporting. Unless the person is someone who has had experience with mental illness or who is naturally very tactful, the information may be passed on inaccurately.

Lucy related later that she would not have had the maturity to deal with the situation earlier in her life. Mental illness makes us fearful; we lose our objectivity. Most of us cannot overcome the temptation to see mental illness as permanent. Our best friends will be careful of their conversation lest information be distorted. The teller is often expressing his or her fear, guilt, or shame.

The family is helped greatly when friends do not exaggerate or become doomsayers. Today the record of treatment is very good. Patients do recover; I did. Nobody knows that another person will not recover.

Finally, pray daily for your depressed friend. I am so grateful to all my friends who were praying for me. I know God was at work in my depression, and I also believe the prayers of my friends were helpful toward this end. Since God in the Scriptures asks for our prayers, God obviously chooses to work through them. In this sense, we are God's collaborators.

## *Lucy speaks*

*Friends*

As Bill's condition deteriorated, it became increasingly difficult to answer the questions of our friends. None of them had ever had a similar experience. So when they kept asking for specifics, I just said, "They are treating him, and there is no change." I kept what someone later described as a closed mouth. I continued the steady pace and believed that I and mine were in the Everlasting Arms.

During this time, hospital visitors were not helpful and that is why we had the "no visitors" rule. I had an overall picture of the hospital stay and had to be aware of the future. Non-family members could not relate to Bill; he did not want to see them, and he would not communicate with them. It was far too frustrating even to try to explain to them what was happening. Nobody except someone who has recovered from mental illness could have understood the situation. When Bill was in the unit for the severely disturbed, even such a person could not have helped.

None of those to whom I have referred in this book were bad people. Their intentions were good and they were and remain good friends. Those were ticklish times for me, and I may or may not have been sufficiently sensitive.

Many people were very helpful to me and to the children. I believe the most helpful were those who had themselves been involved in a socially unacceptable trauma. They had been there, just as we now have been there, and so we in turn can be helpful to others. Such friends are those whom Henri Nouwen calls "the wounded healers." One of our friends shared with me her song of God as "the climbing coach." This imagery still helps us as it shows that God's wisdom and strength, makes it possible for us to endure and to climb back up without fatigue.

When I would say to some, "There is nothing to be done now but to pray for Bill's recovery," I knew they were already praying. This focus on prayer helped me to be more intentional and detailed in my own intercessory prayers. To some of our very intimate friends, I could say, "This is awful. I can't explain it all to you, but nothing except death could be worse." What a gift friends are! Their expressed concerns were much appreciated.

Knowing I was stressed, a woman at work begged me to take time off. She didn't have any details of Bill's condition but still her thoughtful concern was very comforting. I did take a short time off and that was all I needed. Actually with the outcome so uncertain, I preferred to juggle the job with the illness at that time because I knew that, whatever the outcome, I might need days off later, and I did. I appreciated any spiritual comfort and some said such truly loving things to me. They encouraged me in my faith so that I could hang on. I relied on my past experience of deliverance to see me through. I had good reason to have faith because I had many memories that caused me much gratitude.

## Bill speaks

### The Clergy

When you who are pastors call on your depressed parishioners, read the Bible to them, but with cautious selecting. Depressed people are quick to read judgment on themselves in Bible passages, even in those where it would have to be read in. Particularly use the Psalms that touch on depression. Psalm 88 is an example; it is a psalm obviously written by a depressed person (see page 72 in chapter four). All the symptoms of depression are recognizable in it. Yet the psalmist continued his struggle with God. His agitation was expressed dialogically in prayer rather than in an introverted monologue. I stress the Psalms because they give depressed people something to identify with. In the Psalms that express depressed feelings, there is no judgment.

As stated above, use the Scriptures with great care because the depressed person may read judgment even into good news. For example, suppose you read about the wonderful things God gives to those who love God, believe in God, and trust God. The depressed person will immediately miss the good news and will instead question whether he or she really loves God, believes in God, or trusts God, and will answer the question negatively. With the Psalms this is much less likely to occur because conditions regarding God's favor are rarely given and the feelings that the depressed knows all too well are expressed. It is easy then to go from the Psalms into prayer.

Pray with the depressed person for healing. Make specific petitions in this regard. Through your prayers, try to give some glimmer of hope through God. Stress the unconditional nature of God's love for the depressed person and the offer of God's complete forgiveness for every possible sin in their life. If your depressed parishioner is willing to talk, let the person talk about his or her depressed feelings. Then go from feelings to the thoughts behind the feelings. Help them to assess the rationality of those thoughts and to reject those that are irrational. Then help them create rational thoughts to replace them. Learn the rudiments of cognitive behavioral therapy, through being taught by a CBT therapist, attending workshops on the subject, or reading books about it. Then incorporate these ideas into your pastoral counseling.

Albert Ellis's book, *How to Stubbornly Refuse to Make Yourself Miserable about Anything—Yes, Anything!* (Secaucus, NJ: Lyle Stuart, 1988), is a good book on CBT and was helpful to me. CBT concepts fit into pastoral counseling quite naturally. For instance, you can use Psalm 42:11, "Why are you cast down, O my soul, and why are you disquieted within me? Hope in God; for I shall again praise him, my help and my God," with your parishioner as a biblical form of CBT. In other words, like the psalmist, one can learn to argue with their depressed thoughts and substitute thoughts of hope for them.

If you suspect repressed anger in the depressed person, assist him or her in expressing it. Give permission to let it out. Tell the person that there is nothing wrong with anger because it is part of God's nature and we are created in God's image. Role playing is a good way to allow someone to express anger. Here, of course, you are using the well-known principles of interpersonal psychotherapy in their pastoral counseling context. It can be quite helpful.

In role playing, it works best if you take the role of the parishioner first because this is the role you know best. The parishioner can take the role of the person with whom he or she is angry. In your role playing, model how to express angry feelings toward this person. Then reverse roles so that you take the role of the offending person whom by now you know more about, and the depressed person can see if he or she can follow your role modeling and express angry feelings. This will not be easy and you will need to encourage your parishioner. Again, using the Psalms that express anger may help the depressed person to identify and feel more accepted in the expression of feelings. The Bible gives us permission to express angry feelings.

If your parishioner is seeing a psychiatrist or a psychotherapist, let him or her know of your pastoral involvement with the client and ask how you can be helpful. Work with your depressed person's psychiatrist or psychotherapist, if possible, in a team approach. If your parishioner is not being treated by anyone, have a name or two to recommend, and encourage the person to make an appointment. A psychiatrist can prescribe the needed medication, which can make a big difference in the person's recovery. If need be, you can offer to make the appointment for the person and accompany him or her to the first appointment. Do anything you can to get depressed persons to the help they need!

I recall talking with a man at a workshop who told me that his psychiatrist had finally, after many attempts, settled on a medication that helped the man in his depression. But he still was not cured. He was not getting any psychotherapy from the psychiatrist, which is not unusual. In fact, it is becoming more and more the case that busy psychiatrists are settling for administering the proper medication. However, people need both medication and psychotherapy or pastoral counseling in their depressions. I encouraged the man to get into a regular therapy program with a pastoral counselor or a clinical psychologist.

Of course, in all of your work with depressed people, work also with the family, soliciting their help in getting their loved one to the care he or she needs. The family needs your pastoral care also. They are under much stress and need your ministry to help them live with their stress as positively and hopefully as possible.

## LEARNING MORE ABOUT DEPRESSION

In this section of the chapter, I will tell more about the stigma of mental illness and its connection to many suicides.

When the possibility of my going to the mental hospital became real, Lucy, who had just been through the experience of having me in the general hospital for three weeks, did not relish the idea. She said, "If you go to the mental hospital, that may be the end of your career." My response was one typical of a depressed person, "My career is over anyhow."

Lucy was reflecting the stigma that our society has against mental illness. In my depressed thinking, there was no threat at all in being considered mentally ill because I believed I was a goner anyway. But rationally, Lucy had a point: Would I be wanted at the seminary after this, particularly if I had been hospitalized? I had already been relieved of my teaching duties due to the pneumonia. Now that leave would have to be extended. What would we tell them? Pneumonia is much easier to give as a reason than depression.

Even then I believe my mind recalled the Thomas Eagleton affair, which is within the memory of many adults. Eagleton was the vice-presidential candidate on the Democratic ticket with George McGovern in 1972. Someone leaked to the press that Eagleton had previously suffered from depression and had received shock treatments for it. Acting on some poor advice, McGovern asked Eagleton to withdraw from the ticket. Now that I have been where Eagleton was, I react far more strongly to McGovern's decision than I did at the time. Now I believe it was a decision that stamped the stigma of mental illness deeply into our society.

People don't often have many people to turn to in time of trouble. We are oriented to hear about good times. "Tell me about the good, not the bad" often seems to be the message. There are even fewer people to turn to when the problem is mental illness. "Nobody knows how to talk to me," lamented a wife whose husband had recently become mentally ill.

## Not Ashamed

A man who had also suffered from clinical depression wrote to me after reading my article in *The Journal of Pastoral Care* (see page

124 of the list for further reading). He said, "You are not ashamed of a human condition, which you would wish nobody else to share but which has shaped you in the near present. Neither, thanks to the bold example of the likes of you, am I. We all confess this, not with pride, but with the gratitude of a family of survivors."

## THE STIGMA AND SUICIDE

Because depression is so widespread, it is time we challenged the stupidity of this stigma. Perhaps if we called depression a brain disease, which in many respects it is, that would move it more toward the physical and hence make it more acceptable. Because of the stigma, families have often tended to cover up for their depressed member—to "hide" him or her. Therefore the depressed person doesn't get to the needed help as soon as possible. The condition, consequently, grows worse.

This delay is most serious because of the possibility of suicide. As I wrote this chapter, Washington D.C. was stunned by the suicide of Vincent Foster, President Clinton's legal adviser. Although he left no suicide note, bits and pieces of a note he had recently scribbled showed a man in deep depression. He was too sensitive to live in the calloused atmosphere of political Washington. In this atmosphere, he said it was considered a sport in the press to ruin people. Several critical editorials regarding his work by the *Wall Street Journal* added to his pain. The person who might have saved him, had he gone to him, was his friend from boyhood, President Clinton. He couldn't go to him, he thought, because he believed that because of his recent supposed "failures," he was letting the president down. So in a terribly depressing moment, his "crazy thinking" led him to put a bullet through his head. A tragic loss!

Just prior to his suicide, Mr. Foster had returned to his alma mater law school in Arkansas to give the commencement address. In that address, he gave a clue to the approaching tragedy. "Reputation," he said to the graduates, "was all. . . . I can't make this point too strongly. Dents to the reputation in the legal profession are irreparable" ("The Suicide," *The New Yorker*, August 9, 1993, page 42). The critical newspaper editorials in the *Wall Street Journal* may have led him to believe that his good reputation was lost. Then, according to his belief, he would have nothing left.

Suicides like that of Vincent Foster occur far too often. The rate is unnecessarily high and probably could be cut in half. Ted Arneson, in his depression, made a suicide attempt and failed. Now he is dedicating himself, as a person with some power in the Minnesota health scene, to cutting this figure in the state in half during his lifetime.

Ted is unusual in that he has come out openly about his depression. By doing so he may be jeopardizing his position in the business world. He has said that as a businessperson, he wonders what would happen if, for example, he needed another loan, which has happened in the past, to operate his business.

In the depressed thinking of the suicidal person, there is a growing conviction that everybody, family included, would be better off without him or her. Suicide can be a way of solving the problem of his or her misery that is also "altruistic." Even a depressed child can feel this way. A twelve-year-old boy confided to his counselor, "I'm not happy and making no one else happy, so I might as well end it."

## FAMILIES THAT SURVIVE SUICIDE

The family of a depressed person who chose suicide may find that their support system can be very thin. Most people feel uncomfortable in their presence, not knowing what to say. However, special support groups for suicide survivors are now available through social agencies and some churches. There people can talk about suicide without being judged.

Our family knows the difficulty of getting support from friends after a suicide in the family because we have been there. One of our daughters took her life after being hospitalized for the psychotic effects of a prepartum depression. After she had made a suicide attempt, her husband convinced her to see a psychiatrist, who hospitalized her. But neither he nor the hospital took enough precautions, and within twenty-four hours she had hung herself on curtain rods that had not been removed from her room. So even though I have stressed the importance of hospitalization for the safety of a depressed person who is suicidal, obviously the hospital is not always a safe place. Therefore it is most important when admitting a depressed person to find out what suicide precautions will be taken.

Fortunately as a family we had friends who could relax in our presence, and we called them repeatedly to visit with us. Usually they were people who had had a similar experience. It takes a certain amount of determination to make such requests for visits, and unfortunately those who have suffered this loss often do not have it. So it is important for those who know them to take the initiative and contact them regardless of how uncomfortable they may feel in doing so. Clergy can take the initiative to organize such visits if the grieving persons are associated with their church.

In the two and a half months that I was in the psychiatric unit, I fantasized over and over again all the possible ways I could take my life, but I never did make the actual effort to try to kill myself; it seemed too far out even for my depressed mind. My psychiatrist confided in my pastoral counselor, Bill Smith, that he was worried that I could be committing psychological suicide by refusing to eat, drink, or participate in any treatment. On several occasions, when the staff became uneasy about me, they had someone sit with me continuously as a suicide watch.

So, again, when admitting a depressed person to a hospital, if you are not satisfied regarding the suicide precautions, find another hospital. Our daughter might have been better cared for in a general hospital than in the private mental hospital to which she was admitted. In a general hospital the door would have been kept open, rather than being closed as it was. There are also usually roommates in a general hospital and nurses coming in and out continuously—which she did not have.

Suicide survivors need to be surrounded by people who are not shocked either by mental illness or suicide, and who do not probe for details to satisfy their morbid curiosity. The stupidity of the stigma regarding mental illness extends also to its sometime result—suicide. And this stigma can prevent suicide survivors from getting the support they so desperately need. We were often surprised by those of our friends who did not come to see us. They probably just couldn't take it. One such person called later to apologize for not coming. He said that at that time he was depressed himself and having suicidal thoughts, and he believed he couldn't risk exposing himself to us.

The grief of suicide survivors is grief to the "nth" power. This is because of the tragic nature of the death and also because we believe such deaths are preventable. Much soul-searching takes place and there is often much guilt. "What could I have done, or not done, to have prevented the death?" Lucy and I both had hindsight awareness of what we might have done had we known the seriousness of our daughter's condition. Unfortunately she lived many miles from us and contacts were only by phone. Even so, we analyzed those phone conversations over and over again, noting clues that we had missed. A comforter who was especially helpful to us described our daughter's death as a psychic malignancy, and that she died from lack of care—which described the situation to us very well. But the agony, of course, in this as well as other suicides, is that it was preventable.

One of the greatest suicide preventers is surveillance. Very few commit suicide when they are with someone. If this surveillance cannot be provided at home, this would give a reason to hospitalize the depressed person. If a hospital is alert to its responsibilities, it can establish many controls that would make it virtually impossible for a patient to end his or her life.

# EPILOGUE

## *Thanks for Everything*

 As the six chapters in this book show, Bill completely recovered from his clinical depression as well as the milder situational depression that occurred later. However, the leukemia first diagnosed in 1990 was not healed. After four and a half productive years, his health suddenly declined, and on February 21, 1995, Bill died. His funeral on February 25 was both a sad farewell and a joyous celebration of his life.

Wife, family, and friends are grieving over the loss of his presence. His sense of fun and his phenomenal energy would never have foreshadowed his depression. No exact cause was ever determined for either the leukemia or the depression. Nothing prepared us for it. With the help of physicians from many departments of the University of Minnesota School of Medicine and many others, he fought his condition determinedly. We have the comfort that all that could have been done for him was done. He said repeatedly to his pastoral counselor, Bill Smith, that he was especially thankful to die able to express his faith and love for his creator and comforter. And so many people have expressed beautifully to the family that they had received from Bill a deeper knowledge of God.

When Bill and I wrote this book, he was functioning well and living a normal life. Depression can take people to the borderland of hell, as it did him. Bill knew that God can bring others through it, as God did with him, and that is why writing this book was so important for him. There is help for depression. Bill knew that underneath everything are the Everlasting Arms and that in all things God is working for good.

Although Bill was not depressed the last years of his life, he did have "down" moments. For example, he had a wound in his foot that necessitated walking with a cane. The wound was slow to heal and Bill felt discouraged. When something like that happened, Bill resorted to CBT. He evaluated his thought, saw that it was doing him no good, and then tossed it out and gave his mind a positive thought, such as the idea that God was using the experience for his spiritual growth.

By telling depressed persons they are loved as they are, the gospel speaks directly to their low self-image. From the gospel they learn that if the perfect God loves them as they are, they must in some sense be OK. If a pastor or some concerned layperson calls and offers a comforting prayer or a word from the Bible, the depressed person will usually feel better. Then the pastor or layperson can leave the depressed person with some other helpful Bible verses to read when he or she is alone.

When Bill and I looked back on his depression, we realized it had one value, namely that life afterward was so much more precious and enjoyable because of the contrast. The opposite of the depressed state of mind is peace of mind, and for years Bill had that. Life is a gift from God, perhaps the basic gift. When it is coupled with peace, it is God's great blessing.

After Bill was released from the hospital, he was required to take Prozac for six months as a precaution. At the end of that period, he stopped taking the drug. Whether it did any good, we did not know because he was already well to start with after the nine ECT treatments.

We had forty-nine years of marriage and our life together kept getting better all the time. Bill retired in the spring of 1990, shortly after his release from the hospital. It was a retirement based on age. To give us more time together, I decided voluntarily to retire at the beginning of 1994.

Writing this book about Bill's depression brought it all back for both of us. Reliving it brought a great sense of gratitude that Bill was no longer depressed. We supposed that because we were at peace with it, we had a readiness to let go of the past. This came from the experience of coping with the present—even when the present was not overwhelmingly lovely. Difficult situations help people not to romanticize the past or present. We moved on to the future, more convinced by hope through experience than ever before. God is good!

In no way can our family deny or forget the past, nor can we assume that the future holds only pleasantries. We know that we may have to travel rough terrain again. Lately some of our old friends have been experiencing difficulties and we cannot be sure of positive outcomes. Yet we need to be just as prepared to meet good results. If we undermine our ability to accept good in the future and allow our memories to destroy a positive past and the learning that comes from it, we are not trusting God, who is always ready to bless us in our experiences. We have the power to live positively in that tension.

Being true to one's self, in touch with one's feelings, and able to lay those feelings beside the Word of God does not mean easy growth. As one matures as a person, the task is not easier. We trust God more, but our self-awareness is keener. To our dismay, we see ourselves as wanting ease and good names, and perhaps even as enjoying others' hardships. The expression "muscular Christians" is not just words. We build and rebuild constantly, exercising and expanding our beliefs. In Bill's case of clinical depression, a chemical imbalance took place. He could not work it out. Others carried him on their faith. When he was cured, he was again able to believe and work in hope. Long ago John Bunyan wrote *Pilgrim's Progress*, showing that the key to getting us out of trouble was God's promises seen in the assurance of the resurrection.

Our experience has led us to this conclusion: In the light of our having experienced healing of mind, body, and spirit, an attitude of positiveness, though seemingly naive when put to the test, can help us to achieve the positive. Bill's physical health was in many ways the result of his having and following a positive attitude. Without hope, why eat nutritious food, rest, or exercise? Although none of those activities comes with a guarantee, the hedging of bets for the positive makes sense. The factors that lead to mental, spiritual, and physical health are so complex that we cannot say that one thing or another is the cause of good results. Even in the midst of today's plethora of information, we still know that the final result resides with God. "Unless the LORD builds the house, those who build it labor in vain" (Psalm 127:1).

When Bill broke one of the bones of his spine in a freak accident, he was able to tolerate negative feelings about his health without feeling sorry for himself. He was able to use his mind constructively while his body was "laid up." He mastered the computer and that helped him to accomplish complex tasks easily compared to former times.

As his caretaker during this time, I had to adjust to the ups and downs of this status. Sometimes I was overwhelmed with the emotional repercussions that accompany caring for a sick person. Our experience was reinforced with a large "must": We must be honest with each other, withhold no negative feelings, and resolve all conflicts. Some conflicts have a past history; those in particular have to be resolved if people are to go on in hope. The Bible was a great help to both of us in our problems and in our relationship.

Our four adult children and a grandson have greatly enriched our lives. Perhaps of all Bill and I treasured, they are the most precious. They are very individual in their lives. Their talents and educations vary widely. All four children have married unique people whose accomplishments we also take pride in. We have been the beneficiaries of their broad perspectives. We have learned much from them. Teaching, nursing, woman's wilderness expertise, accounting, home construction, and music are their choices. Their personal charms are great.

So now five of Bill's birthdays and two other books later, we were pleased to know that this book we wrote on Bill's depression was ready to be published. Bill's book *Christian*

*Caregiving*, a commentary on the book of Job with an emphasis on caregiving, drawn from insights from Job, was begun before Bill became ill and was finished afterward. A second book that Bill and I wrote together, *Nine Challenges for Parents*, was begun before the illness. It was published in December 1993. In that book we shared some of the insights we gained together in being parents.

For the five years following Bill's recovery, we were able to live with a joy that was very satisfying. Bill was able to go back to what he very much enjoyed, particularly speaking to groups, especially clergy.

Together we gave workshops on such subjects as spiritual growth, a Christian approach to conflict management, and a biblical approach to parenting. Working together on these was a satisfying experience as we seemed to complement each other very well. Bill did short presentations on the workshop topic and I prepared specific exercises for people to do when they broke up into small groups.

Bill's chronic myelomonocytic leukemia, said to be incurable by medical standards, held steady for many years and did not interfere with his normal functioning until shortly before he died. For this, of course, we were very grateful.

Our friends in our age group are like family to us and have grown along with us. We have lost some of them to death, and this has been a great loss to us because we were bonded very closely. Over the years, we have shared the significant passages of life with them, and we will never recapture the closeness in other relationships that we had with them because we cannot share such long experiences together. But Bill and I continued to bond with others as we shared with them experiences and knowledge that made us aware of our common humanity.

Right now it is spring again. Every spring brings its own reasons for gratitude. I am thankful that I have been able to experience all that I have. Earth and the environment were precious to Bill and are to all of us in his family. Each new planting time reminds us of the hope that out of seeds from the dying plant comes new life.

This spring is especially poignant because of Bill's death, but we know that death is not the end, but a new beginning. "What is sown is perishable, what is raised is imperishable" (I Corinthians 15:42).

Our family's gratitude to God increases as we inspect the wonder of the world around us and rejoice in God's promise of victory over death. The words carved into a Norwegian tombstone speak for us, *"Takk for alt,"* thanks for everything!

# For Further Reading

Ashbrook, James B. "Psychopharmacology and Pastoral Counseling: Medication and Meaning." *The Journal of Pastoral Care* 49, no. I (Spring 1995): 5.

*Rev. Ashbrook, Senior Scholar in Religion and Personality at Garrett Evangelical Theological Seminary, asserts that emerging therapeutic approaches of psychiatrists and pastoral therapists need to combine medication for biochemical processes and meaning for framing experience.*

Burns, David D., M.D. *Feeling Good.* New York: W. Morrow, 1980.
_____. *The Feeling Good Handbook.* New York: W. Morrow, 1989.

*These self-help books for depression are based on cognitive therapy, a known effective treatment for depression. The Feeling Good Handbook is a supplement containing useful self-help exercises.*

Ciarrocchi, Joseph W. *A Minister's Handbook of Mental Disorders.* Mahwah, NJ: Paulist Press, 1993.

*The author encourages clergy "to educate themselves regarding mental health issues and interact assertively with mental health professionals" (p. 8). This is a solid resource book for pastors.*

Copeland, Mary Ellen. *The Depression Workbook: A Guide to Living with Depression and Manic Depression.* Oakland, CA: New Harbinger Publishers, 1992.

*A popular self-help book for anyone.*

Ellis, Albert. *How to Stubbornly Refuse to Make Yourself Miserable about Anything—Yes, Anything!* Secaucus, NJ: Lyle Stuart, 1988.

*A good source of information about cognitive behavioral therapy and how to use it to overcome depression.*

Hulme, William E. "Ministry in Depression." *The Journal of Pastoral Care* 48, no. I (Spring 1994): 91-94.

Klein, Donald F., M.D., and Paul H. Wender, M.D. *Understanding Depression.* New York: Oxford University Press, 1993.

*Two authorities on clinical depression define it as a biological illness. This is a brief but comprehensive book covering the symptoms, causes, diagnosis, and treatment of depression.*

Kramer, Peter D. *Listening to Prozac.* New York: Penguin Books, 1994.

*A very readable book by a professor of psychiatry. He gives an interesting history of the development of antidepressant medications, tells why and how they work, raises ethical questions about their use, and identifies key points of stress in human life that bear on depression.*

Manning, Martha. *Undercurrents.* San Francisco: HarperSanFrancisco, 1994.

*The self-told story of a psychotherapist's battle with a deadly depression. Robert Coles comments on this book: "A wonderfully candid, lucid, and engaging account of a talented, knowing psychotherapist's struggle with a tenacious, even life-threatening depression." This is a classic story of the healer who needs healing.*

Papolos, Demetri F., and Janice Papolos. *Overcoming Depression.* New York: Harper & Row, 1987.

*Recommended by a cognitive behavior therapist.*

Seligman, Martin E. P. *Helplessness: On Depression, Development, and Death.* New York: W. H. Freeman, 1992.

*A nationally known research psychologist who coined the phrase "learned helplessness" provides a unique perspective on depression. Though a self-disclaimed biblical scholar, he includes some concordance research in his books. Also by Seligman:*
> *Learned Optimism.* New York: A. A. Knopf, 1991.
> *What You Can Change & What You Can't.* New York: A. A. Knopf, 1994.

Styron, William. *Darkness Visible.* New York: Random House, 1990.

*The story of a famous American author's own battle with depression.*

Yapko, Michael D. *When Living Hurts.* New York: Brunner/Mazel, 1988.

*A psychologist takes a wide view of depression providing a thorough understanding of it. He is especially helpful in distinguishing hurtful life experiences from clinical depression.*